Banking and Finance

BUSINESS ENGLISH

Christine Johnson

Longman

FINANCIAL TIMES
World business newspaper.

Pearson Education Limited
Edinburgh Gate
Harlow
Essex CM20 2JE
England

First published 2000

ISBN 0 582 328438

Set in 10/12.5pt Apolline, 10.5/12.5pt MetaPlus

Printed in Spain by Mateu Cromo, S.A. Pinto, Madrid

www.market-leader.net

Acknowledgements

We are indebted to the following for permission to reproduce copyright material:
British Airways for extract from table 'Summary Group Profit & Loss Account' audited for the year 31 March 1998. Company Accounts on British Airways Website www.british-airways.com; European Central Bank for extracts from 'Organisation of the European System of Central Banks (ESCB)' on www.ecb.int/about/absorg.htm © European Central Bank; Financial Times Limited for adapted extracts from 'Plenty of business for banks' in FINANCIAL TIMES 26.6.1998; 'Growth's financial complications' in FINANCIAL TIMES 5.11.1997; 'Launch is scheduled at a critical time for industry' in FINANCIAL TIMES 24.6.1998; 'Easy money' in FINANCIAL TIMES 20.2.1999; 'Survival of the biggest' in FINANCIAL TIMES 13.1.1998; 'Dollar's boost' in FINANCIAL TIMES 9.1.1999; Yen drops on reports of US pressure' in FINANCIAL TIMES 11.2.1999; Tietmeyer sparks euro profit taking' in FINANCIAL TIMES 9.3.1999; 'Worries over IMF loan delay' in FINANCIAL TIMES 22.2.1999; 'Brazil's high rates bring recession' in FINANCIAL TIMES 22.2.1999; 'Trade surplus narrows' in FINANCIAL TIMES 1.3.1999; 'Uganda close to big hydroelectric deal' in FINANCIAL TIMES 11.2.1999; 'Consortium to fund Croatia's motorways' in FINANCIAL TIMES 11.2.1999; 'Manufacturing price falls fuel fears of deflation' in FINANCIAL TIMES 5.1.1999; 'Profit from the prophets' in FINANCIAL TIMES 22.2.1999; first-e the internet bank; Midland Bank plc for extracts from 'A Guide to Making International Payments through Midland' in ELECTRONIC BANKING, Midland Bank plc September 1996 and 'Guide to exporting and importing' booklet (1994); National Westminster Bank plc for extracts from MONDEX INFORMATION BOOKLET (1994); News International Syndication for an extract from 'It's all for One and One for all' by Roger Anderson in THE SUNDAY TIMES 31.5.1998 © Times Newspapers 1998; Schroder Unit Trust Ltd for extracts from the articles 'Trading on Teamwork' in an early 1999 issue of SCHRODER INVESTOR and 'Schroder Japan Growth Fund plc' by James Salter in SCHRODER INVESTOR June 1999.

Illustration acknowledgements

Nick Baker for 73

Photo acknowledgements

We are grateful to the following for their permission to reproduce copyright photographs:
Powerstock Photo Library for page 29 and Telegraph Colour Library for page 8.
The cover photograph has been kindly supplied by Robert Harding Picture Library

Project Managed by Chris Hartley

Contents

Part 1 **PERSONAL BANKING**

    Unit 1   Designed for the Internet   **4**

    Unit 2   Electronic cash   **8**

    Unit 3   The One account   **12**

Part 2 **CORPORATE BANKING**

    Unit 4   Companies and their banks   **16**

    Unit 5   Company accounts   **20**

    Unit 6   Globalisation   **24**

Part 3 **THE BANKING INDUSTRY**

    Unit 7   The European Central Bank   **28**

    Unit 8   Profitable banks   **32**

    Unit 9   Bank mergers   **36**

Part 4 **INTERNATIONAL BANKING**

    Unit 10   Currency markets   **40**

    Unit 11   Sending money overseas: priority payments   **44**

    Unit 12   Foreign trade   **48**

Part 5 **WORLD ECONOMICS**

    Unit 13   Economic reports   **52**

    Unit 14   Project finance   **56**

    Unit 15   Deflation   **60**

Part 6 **INVESTMENTS**

    Unit 16   The work of a fund manager   **64**

    Unit 17   Share review   **68**

    Unit 18   Profit from the prophets   **72**

Glossary   **76**

Key   **84**

Check Tests   **92**

Check Tests Key   **96**

Designed for the Internet

Before you read

Discuss these questions

1 Which of the following does your bank offer?

   a) branches in every town   **b)** telephone banking services   **c)** internet banking?

2 How do you usually manage your account?

   a) visit the local branch   **c)** by phone

   b) by post   **d)** on the Internet

3 Would you like to change the way you bank? Why?/Why not?

Reading tasks

A Identifying general content

Read the text on the opposite page about an internet bank and match the sub-headings (**1–6**) with the extracts (**a–f**).

1 transfer cash out conveniently & easily   *extract e*

2 designed for the Internet, not the high street

3 opening an account is simple – it only takes an instant

4 manage your finances the easy way

5 high interest rates

6 your money is safe with us

B Understanding details

Mark these statements true (T) or F (false) according to the text. Find the part of the text that gives the correct information.

first-e ...

1 has a prestige high street address in every town.   *F*

2 offers high interest rates on savings.

3 lets you open an account without the need for paper documents.

4 allows you to transfer funds on-line.

5 doesn't make any bank charges to its customers.

6 takes 3 days to transfer funds from one first-e account to another.

7 offers customers a cheque book.

8 protects customer security using encryption technology.

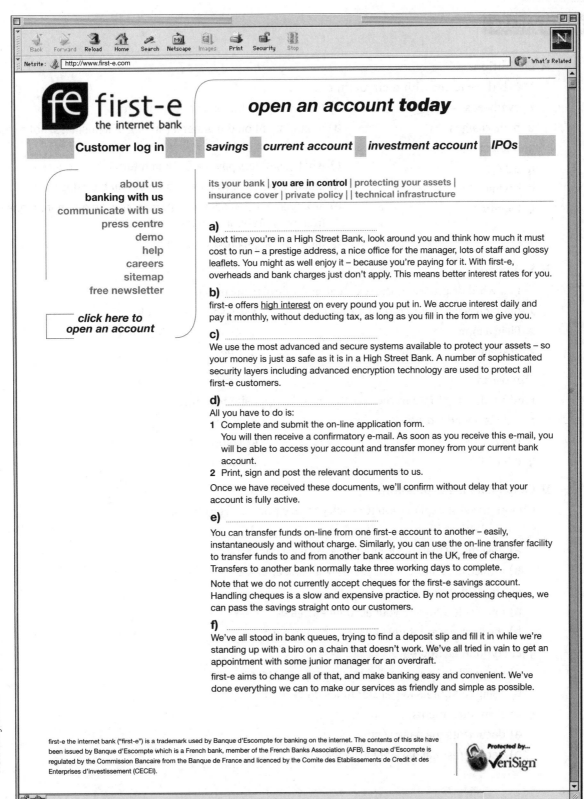

fe first-e
the internet bank

open an account today

Customer log in | savings | current account | investment account | IPOs

about us
banking with us
communicate with us
press centre
demo
help
careers
sitemap
free newsletter

**click here to
open an account**

its your bank | **you are in control** | protecting your assets |
insurance cover | private policy | | technical infrastructure

a)
Next time you're in a High Street Bank, look around you and think how much it must cost to run – a prestige address, a nice office for the manager, lots of staff and glossy leaflets. You might as well enjoy it – because you're paying for it. With first-e, overheads and bank charges just don't apply. This means better interest rates for you.

b)
first-e offers high interest on every pound you put in. We accrue interest daily and pay it monthly, without deducting tax, as long as you fill in the form we give you.

c)
We use the most advanced and secure systems available to protect your assets – so your money is just as safe as it is in a High Street Bank. A number of sophisticated security layers including advanced encryption technology are used to protect all first-e customers.

d)
All you have to do is:
1 Complete and submit the on-line application form.
   You will then receive a confirmatory e-mail. As soon as you receive this e-mail, you will be able to access your account and transfer money from your current bank account.
2 Print, sign and post the relevant documents to us.

Once we have received these documents, we'll confirm without delay that your account is fully active.

e)
You can transfer funds on-line from one first-e account to another – easily, instantaneously and without charge. Similarly, you can use the on-line transfer facility to transfer funds to and from another bank account in the UK, free of charge. Transfers to another bank normally take three working days to complete.

Note that we do not currently accept cheques for the first-e savings account. Handling cheques is a slow and expensive practice. By not processing cheques, we can pass the savings straight onto our customers.

f)
We've all stood in bank queues, trying to find a deposit slip and fill it in while we're standing up with a biro on a chain that doesn't work. We've all tried in vain to get an appointment with some junior manager for an overdraft.

first-e aims to change all of that, and make banking easy and convenient. We've done everything we can to make our services as friendly and simple as possible.

From *www.first-e.com*

Vocabulary tasks

A Definitions

Match these terms with their definitions.

1 overheads
2 bank charges
3 interest rate
4 assets
5 savings
6 overdraft

a) money kept in the bank to earn interest

b) money spent on the general running of a business, not related to producing goods or selling services

c) what customers pay the bank in return for its services

d) amount the bank will pay customers on their deposits

e) arrangement that allows customers to take out more money from their account than they have put in

f) funds belonging to an individual

B Synonyms

Find a word or phrase in the text that has a similar meaning.

1 put money into your account *deposit*
2 fill in a form
3 present

4 as soon as possible
5 money in your account
6 free

C Opposites

Find a word or phrase in the text that has the opposite meaning.

1 old-fashioned *advanced*
2 risky
3 difficult

4 cheap
5 complicated
6 impersonal

D Understanding expressions

Choose the best explanation for each of these phrases from the text.

1 glossy leaflets
   a) advertising material printed on expensive paper ✓
   b) attractive plants used to decorate a bank or office

2 we accrue interest daily
   a) interest is added to your account each day
   b) the bank earns interest on your account each day

3 encryption technology
   a) writing data in a code that people can not access
   b) using computers to transfer funds quickly

4 relevant documents
   a) documents the bank sent
   b) documents that have been signed

5 deposit slip

    a) envelope you put money in when you pay cash into your account

    b) form you complete when you pay money into your account

6 in vain

    a) taking a lot of time and effort

    b) trying hard but without success

E Collocations

Match the verbs and nouns as they occur in the text.

1 offer	**a)** funds
2 deduct	**b)** interest
3 fill in	**c)** an account
4 protect	**d)** a form
5 open	**e)** assets
6 submit	**f)** cheques
7 transfer	**g)** tax
8 accept	**h)** an application

F Complete the sentence

Use an appropriate phrase from Exercise E to complete each sentence.

1 The bank *offers interest* of 5% on all deposits.

2 The customer was asked to .... and hand it in at the desk.

3 With internet banking, it is possible to .... on-line from one account to another.

4 In order to reduce costs, many internet banks don't ....

5 To apply for a job, or to open a new account, you have to ....

6 Many people .... at a bank when they start their first job.

7 Interest is paid gross, which means that the bank does not ....

8 Customers needn't worry about security, the bank uses sophisticated encryption technology to .... their ....

Over to you

1 Make a list of the advantages and disadvantages of internet banking. Discuss it with a partner.

2 Visit the first-e website at www.first-e.com and see what other information you can get about the bank.

3 Make a comparison between first-e and any bank that offers internet banking services in your country.

Electronic cash

Before you read

Discuss these questions.

1 When you go shopping in your country, how do you pay for goods?

2 List all the payment options you can think of.

3 Which of these ways to pay is most secure from the point of view of avoiding loss or theft of your money?

Reading tasks

A Identifying general content

Match the sub-headings (**1–6**) with paragraphs (**a–f**) in the text on the opposite page.

1 Mondex purse   *a*

2 Mondex point-of-sale device

3 Lock

4 Mondex balance reader

5 Mondex wallet

6 Mondex telephone

B Understanding main points

Mark these statements T (true) or F (false) according to the information in the text. Find the part of the text that gives the correct information.

1 Mondex can be used to pay for goods and services.   *T*

2 Shopkeepers can be paid without delay.

3 You need to sign to authorise payment.

4 To check how much money is stored on your card you have to telephone your bank.

5 You can load money onto your card using a special telephone.

6 Money can be transferred in or out of your bank account 24 hours a day.

7 Mondex can only be used to pay money to businesses such as shops or service providers.

8 A disadvantage is that you cannot record the transactions you have made.

9 You can protect your money from thieves by using a 'lock code'.

Mondex is electronic cash, stored securely in a smart card. For consumers, Mondex offers all the convenience, control and flexibility of cash in the familiar form of a card.

5 Retailers will receive funds immediately without the need for authorisation or settlement when consumers pay for goods and services with a Mondex prepayment card. The receipt of value in a Mondex transaction is as immediate and certain as ordinary cash – but Mondex value can be banked easily at any time of the day or night.

Mondex complements credit and debit cards, delivering new levels of efficiency,
10 cost-savings and marketing opportunities for all retailers and service providers.

a) ....

In the new Mondex payment system, monetary value is stored in an Integrated Circuit (IC) Chip known as the electronic purse. Purses are held by all participants in the system – personal cardholders, retailers, service providers and banks.

15 For personal cardholders the purse will be a standard, plastic IC card. This can be loaded with electronic value via a Mondex telephone – bringing a new dimension in money management and electronic cash transactions – or in much the same way as cash is currently obtained, for example from a cash machine or a bank branch.

b) ....

20 To check how much money remains on their card, all cardholders will receive a Mondex balance reader – a small lightweight device in the form of a key ring.

c) ....

When paying for goods or services, the exact amount is simply transferred from the card to the retailer's purse in a Mondex point-of-sale (POS) device. No PIN, authorisation or signature is
25 required – just like cash.

d) ....

Telephones will be especially adapted to enable cardholders to access their bank account at any time; to withdraw or pay-in value down the telephone line; order and pay immediately for goods and services from a retailer; send and receive money to or from friends and family. For a retailer,
30 a Mondex telephone means that value can be deposited directly into their account at any time of the day and night.

e) ....

The Mondex wallet will make person-to-person payments possible. Electronic cash can be transferred between any Mondex card and a separate purse held in the wallet. The wallet will
35 also read the balance on the card and/or the wallet as well as maintain a log of the last ten transactions.

f) ....

Mondex electronic purses contain a 4-digit 'lock code'. By pressing the lock key on devices such as a wallet or telephone, the cardholder's money is kept secure and their transactions private.

From the *Mondex Information Booklet*, National Westminster Bank plc

Vocabulary tasks

A Word fields

Write these words and phrases in the appropriate columns.

> retailer   purse   convenience   make a payment   bank   withdraw   deposit   cost-savings
> service provider   telephone   POS device   security   reader   flexibility   transfer money

participants	devices	benefits	transactions
retailer	purse	convenience	make a payment
......	......	......	......
......	......	......	......
	......	......	......

B Complete the sentence

Use an appropriate word or phrase from Exercise A to complete each sentence.

1 Electronic money provides more ....*security*..... than cash because the lock function makes it difficult to steal.

2 The .... is used by the retailer to receive payment from customers.

3 A company that offers a service is called a ....

4 When you pay money into your bank account, we say that you make a ....

5 The Mondex system offers .... because it is easy to use. Also the wallet and reader are not heavy to carry.

6 Mondex is used to .... between personal cardholders as well as from consumers to retailers.

C Complete the sentence

Use an appropriate word or phrase from the text to complete each sentence.

1 When you pay by credit card, you must sign the payment slip to a*uthorise*........ the payment.

2 The number 4791 consists of four d................... .

3 Once you have s................... your debts, you no longer owe money.

4 The b................... of my account was £100. I have now paid out £40, so £60 remains.

D Word search

Find a word or phrase from the text that has a similar meaning.

1 amount of money (para 2)   f.*unds*...........

2 adds to (para 3)   c...................

3 ATM (para 5)   c.................. m...................

4 not heavy (para 6)   l...................

5 record (para 9)   l...................

E Collocations

Match these verbs and nouns as they occur in the text.

	money	goods or services	your bank account	the balance of your account
pay for	✗	✓	✗	✗
access				
withdraw				
read				
deposit				
transfer				
check				

F Linking

Match the first half of each sentence with the most appropriate second half.

1 Using the Mondex telephone you can withdraw money

2 Retailers can deposit money

3 Retailers can use the Mondex system to receive payment

4 The wallet can be used to transfer funds

5 Electronic cash is stored

6 You can send money over the telephone

a) in the IC chip which is known as a purse.

b) into their account at any time.

c) to friends and family.

d) from your account.

e) from customers.

f) between any two personal cardholders.

Over to you

1 Imagine you are a banking officer talking to a bank customer. Explain how Mondex works.

2 Either orally or in writing, describe the benefits of the Mondex system for
   a) retailers
   b) consumers

3 Compare smart cards such as Mondex with
   a) credit cards or debit cards
   b) cash

4 Describe a similar payment system which you are familiar with.

The One account

Discuss these questions.

1 What kinds of bank accounts are offered by the banks in your country?

2 What is a mortgage? How do people usually arrange and repay their mortgages?

3 Do you think bank customers are happy with the way their bank accounts and mortgage accounts are handled? What could be done to improve the system?

Reading tasks

A Understanding main points

Mark these statements T (true) or F (false) according to the information in the text on the opposite page. Find the part of the text that gives the correct information.

The One account ...

1 combines savings and debts in the same account. *T*

2 cuts the cost of borrowing.

3 pays higher interest than other accounts.

4 provides you with a chequebook and bank cards.

5 limits the number of withdrawals you can make.

6 offers you an agreed overdraft facility of thousands of pounds.

7 requires you to pay your salary into it.

8 requires that you pay off your mortgage in fixed regular instalments.

9 sets a fixed term for your mortgage repayment.

10 allows you to pay off your mortgage whenever you want.

11 is only offered to married couples.

12 calculates interest on a daily basis.

B Understanding details

A potential customer asks questions about the One account. Find the answers.

1 My house is valued at £50,000. Can I borrow £60,000? *No*

2 My house is valued at £50,000. I need an 80% mortgage. Can I borrow an extra £10,000?

3 I plan to retire in 20 years. Can I have 25 years to pay off my mortgage?

4 I want to pay off some of the capital on my mortgage early. Do you make a charge for this?

5 I want to pay off some of the capital on my mortgage early. Will you credit the repayments immediately?

6 If interest rates go up, does that mean I'll have to pay more?

It's all for One – and One for all

Virgin's new account gathers all the elements of the personal finance jigsaw into one complete picture, explains **Roger Anderson**

Most people will spend most of their life owing other people money. They do not realise that 5 they can save money (sometimes quite a lot) by consolidating their income, savings and debts into a single bank account.

This, of course, is not the 10 traditional way that people run their personal finances, with salaries going into one account, savings into another and a completely different arrangement to pay off the mortgage. 15 The One account allows you to put your savings and borrowings together, keeping the cost of your borrowing to a minimum.

When you open a One account, 20 you negotiate an overall borrowing facility that can represent as much as 95% of the value of your home. Thus a couple with a £100,000 house – and needing an 80% mortgage – 25 might set up a loan facility of £95,000, giving them an additional £15,000 to call on when required.

Once the lending facility has been agreed, you can dip into it whenever 30 you want and, equally important, pay it off however you choose. You must satisfy the bank that you will have repaid the debt by the end of an agreed term, such as 25 years. The 35 main proviso is that you must have repaid the debt by the time you retire.

Your salary must be paid into the account and you must pay interest 40 (which is calculated daily) at a current rate. At the same time, the One account is run like an ordinary bank account (you get a chequebook and bank cards and 45 there are no restrictions on the number of withdrawals).

On the face of it, only a fool would put his money into one bank earning interest at, say 6%, and then 50 borrow the same amount from another bank at 10%. But this is precisely what most people are doing – they are funding mortgages at rates much higher than they are 55 getting for their savings. And for much of the time, they are not getting any interest at all on money in their ordinary bank accounts.

Most borrowers have little choice 60 about how to manage mortgage debt, other than to pay regular amounts prescribed by the lender. If they want to pay off capital early, they find that some lenders charge 65 for this, while many lenders will not credit any extra capital repayments until the year end. This means that for most of the year interest is being charged as if for a loan that is bigger 70 than the one that actually exists. Take, for instance, a mortgage of £60,000, repayable over 25 years at an interest rate of 8.55%. Your typical loan repayments would be 75 £490 a month. If, however, your repayments were taken into account the moment they were made, you could repay your loan 11 months early, saving more than £5,000.

80 Where you can really start eating into your debt is by having your salary paid into your mortgage account. As salaries rise – and you can afford to repay more of your debt 85 – the term of what, traditionally, would have been a 25-year mortgage can be cut quite dramatically.

From *The Sunday Times*

Vocabulary tasks

A Complete the sentence

Use an appropriate form of each word in the box to complete the text below.

loan	owe	debt	borrow	repay	lend

Joe took out a ....*loan*.........[1] so that he could buy a car. The car cost £10,000 and the bank agreed to ....[2] him £8,000. About a year later, Joe lost his job and started to worry about his ....[3]. How could he ....[4] it with no salary coming in? Out of the £8,000 that he had originally ....[5], he still ....[6] more than £5,000.

B Word search

Find a word or phrase in the text that has a similar meaning.

1 ongoing opportunity to get extra credit without asking the lender (para 4)

f.*acility*..........

2 period of time in which a loan must be repaid (para 5)

t..................

3 rate of interest which is set at the present time (para 6)

c.................. r..................

4 action of taking money from your bank account (para 6)

w..................

5 money which you deposit with a bank, which earns interest for you (para 7)

s..................

6 if you can do this, you are able to pay for something because you have enough money (para 9)

a..................

C Understanding expressions

Choose the best explanation for each of these words and phrases from the text.

1 consolidating (line 6)
   a) putting everything together ✓
   b) making everything more secure

2 call on (line 27)
   a) to be available
   b) to be agreed by telephone

3 dip into it (line 29)
   a) take all of it at once
   b) take part of it at any time

4 main proviso (line 35)
   a) the main point
   b) an important restriction

5 on the face of it (line 47)
   a) it seems obvious
   b) at the present time

6 prescribed (line 62)
   a) fixed
   b) suggested

7 eating into (line 80)
   a) rapidly reducing
   b) gradually reducing

D Collocations

Match these verbs and nouns as they occur in the text.

1 pay off   **a)** interest

2 earn   **b)** your finances

3 set up   **c)** a mortgage

4 run   **d)** a loan facility

E Complete the sentence

Use an appropriate phrase from Exercise D to complete each of the sentences.

1 He .... of 8% on his account.

2 She wanted to start her own business, so she asked the bank to ....

3 She lost her job and with no regular income it was difficult to ....

4 He was an accountant, so it was not surprising that he was good at ....

F Word search

Find a word in the text that has a similar meaning.

1 salary (para 1)   *income*

2 total (para 4)

3 extra (para 4)

4 pay into (an account) (para 8)

5 pay off (a debt) (para 8)

Over to you

1 Imagine you are a representative from the bank offering the One account. Summarise the key aspects of the One account as if explaining it to a potential customer.

2 Give your opinion about the One account. Would you choose this type of account to help you run your finances?

3 Imagine you are a potential customer. Make a list of questions you would like to ask about the One account. Write a letter to your bank asking them to answer your questions.

Companies and their banks

Before you read

Discuss these questions.

1 What services does a company expect from its bank?

2 What are some of the differences between a loan and an overdraft? Compare your ideas with the definitions in the Key.

3 When offering a loan or an overdraft, a bank usually demands security. What can a customer offer as security?

Reading tasks

Read these two letters from banks to their corporate customers.

Letter A

Dear Mrs Phipps

Re: Retail Banking

On the attached you will find the Bank's proposed Schedule of Charges which will take effect as from 1st January, and will be reviewed annually.

We very much regret that we are unable to continue offering 'free banking' to our customers. This recent change of policy is due to increasing costs, and we feel that if we are to continue to maintain the professional level of personal service that we have always provided to our customers, we must now obtain a contribution to our expenses.

You will note that our charges are below the average levied by other UK banks, as we wish to remain competitive in this market.

The charges will be debited to your account monthly in arrears.

The minimum balance requirement for those accounts which are interest bearing has been reduced from USD 100,000.00 to USD 50,000.00 or currency equivalent. This reduction in the minimum balance requirement will therefore compensate for some of the charges which will have to be paid by yourselves.

If you have any questions concerning the new charges, would you please telephone either myself or my colleague, James Samuel.

Yours sincerely,

Wendy Bracewell

Wendy Bracewell, Account Manager

Letter B

Dear Sirs

Re: Banking facilities

The Bank is pleased to offer John Best Ltd (The Company) banking facilities on the terms referred to below but otherwise subject to normal banking terms and conditions.

Facilities

Withdrawals may be made under the following facilities provided that the total amount of withdrawals at any time shall not exceed the limit.

Overdraft limit: £35,000

Availability

The Bank may at any time discontinue all or any of the facilities and/or may demand repayment of all sums owing. The facilities are due for review in twelve months' time.

Interest rate

Interest on the overdraft facility is to be charged at 2.25% per annum over the Bank's Base Rate as published from time to time.

Fees

An arrangement fee of £120 will be payable.

Security

The repayment of all monies owed in respect of the facilities will be secured by: Business Premises at 44 Park Road, Bristol.

All costs and expenses, as mentioned in the General Terms and Conditions attached to this letter, shall be payable by The Company.

To accept this offer, please arrange for the enclosed copy of this letter to be signed and returned.

Yours faithfully,

Graham Collins

Graham Collins
BRANCH MANAGER

Understanding main points

1 Mark these statements T (true) or F (false) according to the information in Letter A. Find the part of the letter that gives the correct information.

   a) The new charges will remain the same for 12 months. T

   b) The company didn't have to pay bank charges before. F

   c) The bank's policy has changed because the bank wants to be more competitive. T

   d) Other UK banks make lower charges. F

   e) The company will have to pay the charges in advance. F

   f) If the company's account balance is USD 55,000, they will be able to earn interest on this. T

   g) The company will be better off than before because of the extra interest they will earn. F

2 Mark these statements T (true) or F (false) according to the information in Letter B. Find the part of the letter that gives the correct information.

a) According to the letter, the company can overdraw up to a maximum of £35,000.   *T*

b) The period for which the terms of this letter are valid is three years.   *F*

c) The bank has the right to stop the overdraft facility and ask for the money to be paid back before the end of this period.   *T*

d) Other than interest, there will be no charges to pay.   *F*

e) The overdraft facility will be secured by a property.   *T*

f) The contract which the company should sign will be sent at a later date.   *T*

Vocabulary tasks

A Word search

1 Find a word or phrase from Letter A that has a similar meaning.

a) each year or every year (para 1)

a*nnually*........

b) keep something at the same level (para 2)

m..................

c) amount that partly meets costs but does not cover them completely (para 2)

c..................

d) having the same value (para 5)

e..................

2 Find a word or phrase from Letter B that has a similar meaning.

a) go above a specified maximum level (para 2)

e*xceed*.......... a l*imit*.............

b) by the year (para 4)

p.................. a..................

c) fixed amount that has to be paid for a service (para 5)

f..................

d) place where a company carries out its business activities (para 6)

p..................

B Understanding expressions

Choose the best explanation for each of these phrases from the text.

1 monthly in arrears (Letter A, para 4)
  a) payable at the end of the month ✓
  b) payable at the beginning of the month

2 interest bearing accounts (Letter A, para 5)
  a) accounts which are free of interest
  b) accounts which earn interest

3 facilities are due for review (Letter B, para 3)
  a) the money borrowed must be repaid
  b) the bank is going to reconsider the contract

4 Bank's Base Rate (Letter B, para 4)
  a) the key lending rate of banks in Britain
  b) a rate fixed by the bank itself

C Word study: contract language

subject to
This phrase is used to show which rules, regulations or laws have to be followed by the people signing the contract, e.g. *This guarantee is **subject to** the laws of the State of New York.*

provided that
This means the same as *if*, but is very strong, and is common in contracts and means *if and only if*.

shall
Shall is often used instead of *will* in contracts. It is very strong and means that the person signing must do what the contract says.

Match the modal verbs (**1–5**) with their meanings (**a–e**). (Note: not all the answers will be used; one will be used twice)

1 shall
2 shall not
3 may
4 may not
5 will

a) It is allowed under the contract.
b) It is not allowed under the contract.
c) It is an obligation.
d) It is not an obligation.
e) This shows what will be done in the future.

Over to you

1 Imagine you are Mrs Phipps. Write a letter in reply to Letter A, saying that your company is not happy about having to pay charges and you have decided to switch your account to another bank which does not make charges.

2 Imagine you are the Managing Director of John Best Ltd, a company which makes office furniture. Your company has just won a new contract worth £400,000, but in order to carry out the work you need to buy new equipment and recruit extra staff. Write a letter to the bank and ask if you can increase the overdraft facility to £50,000.

Company accounts

Before you read

Discuss these questions.

1 What does the profit and loss account of a company show?
2 If you were the company's bankers, what would you look for when reading this account?
3 What does a company's balance sheet show?
4 What would the company's bankers look for in the balance sheet?

Reading tasks

Read the financial data produced by British Airways and published on the Internet for investors.

SUMMARY GROUP PROFIT AND LOSS ACCOUNT		
AUDITED for the year to March 31, 1998		
£ million	1998	1997
Most of our revenue was earned from our main business, airline operations:	7,881	7,608
Income from other activities earned:	761	751
This gave us total Group turnover of:	8,642	8,359
Our expenses comprised:		
Pay and other employee costs:	2,211	2,248
Depreciation of fixed assets:	551	506
Selling costs:	1,217	1,187
Other operational costs:	4,159	3,872
In total, therefore, our overall Group operating costs were:	8,138	7,813
Deducting this from our Group turnover left a Group operating profit of:	504	546
Other income and charges amounted to:	80	256
The net profit on sale of fixed assets during the year was:	164	20
Net interest payable amounted to:	(168)	(182)
This produced a Group profit before tax of:	580	640
Then we provided for tax totalling:	(133)	(90)
This produced a Group profit after tax of:	447	550
Profit or loss from subsidiaries in which we have a minority interest:	13	3
This left a Group profit attributable to shareholders of:	460	553
From this we allowed for dividends representing a total of:	(176)	(154)
Finally, this left a profit retained in the business of:	284	399

Earnings per share

The standard measure of a company's profitability is calculated by dividing profit attributable to shareholders by the average number of shares.

On this basis, our earnings per share were:	44.7p	55.7p

From www.british-airways.com

SUMMARY GROUP BALANCE SHEET
AUDITED for the year to March 31, 1998

£ million	1998	1997
The Group's fixed assets comprised:		
Our fleet:	7,227	6,337
Property:	1,181	988
Computers, ground and other equipment:	259	263
Investments in other businesses:	388	684
Added together these represented total fixed assets of:	9,055	8,272
Our current assets, mainly money we are owed, our 'cash-in-hand' and stock, represented:	2,245	2,164
Most passengers book and pay for tickets in advance. This money, and amounts owing to creditors that are payable within one year, totalled:	(2,821)	(3,160)
Deducting this gave us net current liabilities of:	(576)	(996)
Adding this to the total fixed assets left us with total assets less current liabilities of:	8,479	7,276
In addition, we owed to creditors amounts due after more than a year including:		
Long-term borrowings of:	(4,978)	(4,034)
We have also made provision for other liabilities and charges:	(180)	(284)
We also had contributions from a minority shareholder in one of our subsidiaries of:	-	26
Thus our assets less liabilities represented:	3,321	2,984
The money invested in the British Airways Group comprised:		
Our share capital, some 1,038.9 million 25p shares:	260	251
Our reserves:	3,061	2,733
	3,321	2,984

Note: If you are not familiar with the terms used in these accounts, do Vocabulary task A: Key terms to check the definitions before attempting the Reading tasks.

A Understanding main points

1 Mark these statements T (true) or F (false) according to the information in the profit and loss account. Find the part of the text that gives the correct information.

   a) The total Group turnover increased slightly on the previous year. *T*

   b) Salaries paid to employees are part of the operating costs.

   c) Interest payable on loans is deducted from the profit after tax.

   d) British Airways sold off some of its assets in 1998.

   e) All the profit is distributed to shareholders.

   f) Earnings per share were lower than in the previous year.

2 Mark these statements T (true) or F (false) according to the information in the balance sheet. Find the part of the text that gives the correct information.

a) The airline's fixed assets include aircraft.   *T*

b) The company had acquired new aircraft since the previous year.

c) The amount of current assets was greater than the amount of current liabilities.

d) Net current liabilities are calculated by deducting current liabilities from total assets.

e) British Airways had issued more than a billion shares at the time of publishing these accounts.

f) British Airways had increased its reserves since the previous year.

Vocabulary tasks

A Key terms

Match these terms with their definitions.

1 turnover	**a)** amount deducted each year from profits to allow for the fact that assets (e.g. equipment) lose their value as they get older
2 operating costs	**b)** total sales during a trading period
3 operating profit	**c)** people the company owes money to, e.g. suppliers
4 depreciation	**d)** past profits not paid out as dividends but retained in the business
5 fixed assets	**e)** short-term assets used in operations, e.g. cash, items held in stock
6 dividend	**f)** money which shareholders have put into the business
7 current assets	**g)** long-term assets owned by the company, e.g. buildings, machinery
8 creditors	**h)** expenses of running a business including salaries, rent, etc. but not including the direct costs of manufacturing
9 current liabilities	**i)** result of deducting the operating expenses from turnover
10 share capital	**j)** part of a company's profits paid to shareholders
11 reserves	**k)** debts that must be paid within one year

B Other terms

The terms below were not used in the British Airways financial data, but are often found in balance sheets. Do you know what they mean? If not, check the Key.

1 debtors

2 long-term loans

C Complete the sentence

Use an appropriate word or phrase from the box to complete the text below.

was earned   allowed   added to this   comprised
deducting this   overall   amounted to   left   totalled

Income from sales		50,000
Income from consultancy		2,500
Total:		**52,500**
Costs:	electricity	500
	phone	800
	rent	10,500
	office supplies	2,400
	advertising	4,200
	other selling costs	2,900
	depreciation	700
Total:		**22,000**
Profit before tax:		**30,500**

Most of my income ..*was earned*..[1] from sales which ....[2] £50,000. ....[3], I received consultancy fees of £2,500. This ....[4] a total turnover of £52,500.

My expenses ....[5]: electricity, phone, office rent and office supplies of £14,200. My advertising and selling costs were £7,100.

I ....[6] £700 for depreciation. Thus, my ....[7] operating costs were £22,000. ....[8] from my turnover ....[9] an operating profit before tax of £30,500.

D Definitions

1 Which word or phrase from the profit and loss account fits each of these definitions?

   a) a standard measure of how profitable the company is *earnings per share*

   b) the total amount of profit which is given out to the shareholders in dividends

2 Which word or phrase from the balance sheet fits each of these definitions?

   a) money which the company has available to spend immediately

   b) goods and supplies which the company has bought but not yet used

   c) money which is set aside for possible future expenses

Over to you

1 Make comparisons between the British Airways figures for 1997 and 1998. Which amounts were higher, better, lower or poorer in 1998? Would the shareholders be satisfied with the 1998 figures, do you think? Why / Why not?

2 Find financial data from other companies, for example from your own company or from another company's annual report. Describe the main points from the data either orally or in writing.

Globalisation

1 Discuss these questions.

  a) What do you understand by the term *global company*? Can you give some examples?

  b) Which companies do you know that have merged recently?

2 Match these terms with their definitions.

1 merger	**a)** when one company gains control of another by buying the majority of its shares
2 acquisition	
3 securities	**b)** when two companies, combine to form one new company
4 restructuring	**c)** a way of assessing the value of a company for shareholders; it includes both dividend payments and the increase in value of the shares over the year
5 total shareholder return (TSR)	
6 earnings per share	**d)** traditional way of assesssing a company's performance by dividing its profits by the number of its shares
	e) investments, especially stocks, shares and bonds
	f) changing the capital base of a company, i.e. the kinds of stocks and shares that comprise the company's capital

A Understanding main points

Mark these statements T (true) or F (false) according to the information in the texts on the opposite page. Find the part of the text that gives the correct information.

1 Most of the big mergers between Swiss companies took place before 1996. *F*

2 The merger of Sandoz and Ciba was good news for the Swiss banks.

3 Investment banks earn a lot of money by giving advice on restructuring.

4 German companies are having to restructure because it is difficult to compete internationally with high costs at home.

5 Companies list on the New York Stock Exchange in order to increase capital at minimum cost.

6 European companies traditionally use earnings per share as a way of estimating value to investors.

7 Valuation techniques such as TSR are only used in the USA.

Text A

Plenty of business for banks

Increasingly, big-ticket deals are being handled by foreign institutions

Switzerland is one of the world's most attractive M&A[1] playgrounds. It has several world-class companies with plenty of cash to spend on acquisitions and a rapidly restructuring corporate finance business.

Until a couple of years ago, the number of mega-deals could be counted on the fingers of one hand. But the market took off after 1996. That was the day Sandoz and Ciba, Switzerland's second and third biggest pharmaceutical companies, announced they were joining forces to create Novartis. Until then, it had been unthinkable that two big Swiss companies, based in the same industry and city, would risk throwing thousands of people out of work by merging.

The idea of one giant Swiss chemical company, or one global insurer, is no longer unimaginable. However, the Ciba/Sandoz press release sent shock waves through the Swiss banking establishment. It revealed that Morgan Stanley had served as bankers for Sandoz and J. P. Morgan had acted for Ciba. The only Swiss bank involved was UBS, and it was given the minor role of banker for the Swiss stock market. Until then, Swiss companies had relied on their Swiss bankers to manage their deals.

The days when Switzerland's most powerful bankers dominated the boards of Switzerland's most powerful companies are over. A banker's presence on a client's board could prevent an investment bank from winning new advisory mandates.

The restructuring of Switzerland's pharma and chemical industries has probably led to more investment banking fees being generated over the past couple of years than had been earned in the past century. More recently, the restructuring has spread to the financial services sector and much of the lucrative advisory work has once again fallen to non-Swiss banks.

FINANCIAL TIMES
World business newspaper.

1 Mergers and acquisitions

Text B

Growth's financial complications

A company that seeks to extend operations around the world needs new financial structures to match, says **Martin Dickson**

When Hoechst, the Frankfurt-based chemicals and drugs group, listed its shares on the New York Stock Exchange, it was a symbolic acknowledgement that a company which aspires to be global in operations must also be global in its approach to finance.

Intensifying international competition and high domestic costs are forcing German businesses – among others – into radical restructuring and a much greater reliance on global securities markets.

For funding their global ambitions, multinationals increasingly accept that to achieve the lowest cost of capital, they have to tap the international markets.

For many non-US companies, a vital element is an equity listing in the US, the world's most liquid and efficient market.

While most European companies still focus on traditional performance measures, US fashions are forcing them to look at new yardsticks, designed to measure the value they are creating for investors, such as total shareholder return (TSR).

'If you're a global company, new valuation techniques are just something you have to take on board,' says Nick Pasricha of Ernst & Young's corporate finance practice, 'because a proportion of your investors are subject to that influence.'

FINANCIAL TIMES
World business newspaper.

B Identifying general content

The split sentences below describe the changes that are taking place as a result of globalisation. Join the first half of each sentence with the most appropriate second half.

1 Global companies
2 Corporate financial services
3 Mergers and acquisitions
4 If you are a global company,
5 Bankers are no longer
6 Large corporations are less likely to

a) are taking place between large companies in the same industry.

b) want to trade on the international securities market.

c) depend on local banks to manage their deals.

d) present on the board of their client companies.

e) are increasingly international.

f) you have to accept the new valuation techniques.

Vocabulary tasks

A Complete the sentence

Use an appropriate word from the texts to complete each of these sentences.

1 When a company makes an official statement that is published in the newspapers, this is called a p.*ress*............. r.*elease*........... . (Text A, para 4)

2 If a company r................... o................... its bank, it means that it trusted it completely and would never use another bank. (Text A, para 4)

3 The directors of a company, the people elected by shareholders to carry on the management of that company, are often called the b................... . (Text A, para 5)

4 Requests to a bank to act for a company are called m................... . (Text A, para 5)

5 When a company offers its shares for purchase by the general public, it gets a l................... on the stock exchange. (Text B, para 4)

6 A l................... stock market is one in which investments can be traded quickly and easily. (Text B, para 4)

B Understanding expressions

Choose the best explanation for each of these words or phrases from the texts.

1 mega-deals (Text A, line 8)
   a) mergers between very large companies   ✓
   b) small, insignificant mergers

2 took off (Text A, line 10)
   a) expanded suddenly
   b) came to an end

3 joining forces (Text A, line 15)
   a) fighting over something
   b) coming together to form a more powerful group

4 lucrative (Text A, line 55)
   a) earning lots of money
   b) earning little money

5 aspires to be (Text B, line 8)
   a) wishes to be
   b) already is

6 tap the international markets (Text B, line 20)
   a) get funds from the international markets
   b) follow the trends of the international markets

7 yardsticks (Text B, line 30)
   a) ways to control something
   b) ways to measure something

8 take on board (Text B, line 36)
   a) resist
   b) accept

C Prepositions

Complete these sentences with an appropriate preposition.

1 Morgan Stanley served ....*as*......... bankers for Sandoz.

2 J. P. Morgan acted .... Ciba.

3 UBS was given the role .... banker for the Swiss stock market.

4 UBS was the only Swiss bank involved .... the deal.

5 Most European companies still focus .... traditional performance measures.

D Opposites

Replace the underlined items with words from the text that have an opposite meaning.

1 Switzerland is one of the world's <u>least</u> attractive M & A playgrounds.   *most*

2 The idea of one giant Swiss chemical company or one global insurer was <u>easy to imagine</u>.

3 The only Swiss bank involved was UBS, and it was only given a <u>major</u> role.

4 Much of the lucrative advisory work has fallen to <u>Swiss</u> banks.

5 Intensifying international competition and <u>low</u> domestic costs are forcing German businesses into radical restructuring.

6 Most European companies focus on <u>new</u> performance measures, such as profitability ratios and earnings per share growth.

Over to you

1 Discuss what role the banks play in corporate financing in your country.

2 Make a list of some of the problems that global companies have nowadays. (You can include both those mentioned in the texts and any others you know about.) Discuss some of the solutions that companies are finding for dealing with these problems.

The European Central Bank

Discuss these questions.

1 What are the different functions of a nation's central bank? If you are not sure, look at the list below. Make sure you know what all the words mean.

- act as banker to the government
- act as banker to the commercial banks
- supervise the banking system
- print and issue banknotes
- maintain financial stability
- conduct foreign exchange operations
- hold and manage foreign exchange reserves

2 Does your country's central bank set interest rates?

A Understanding main points

Read the two short texts on the European System of Central Banks (ESCB) on the opposite page and complete the information below.

1 The ESCB is composed of the *European Central Bank* and the *EU national central banks*.

2 The ECB is run by the ....

3 The organisation of the ECB executive board:

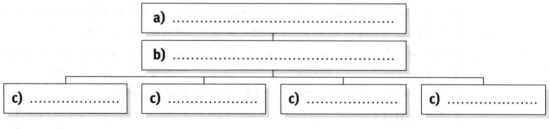

a) ....

b) ....

c) ....   c) ....   c) ....   c) ....

4 The members of the executive board are in charge of:

a) ....
b) ....
c) ....
d) ....
e) ....
f) ....
g) ....

5 The ECB's governing council consists of:

a) ....
b) ....

Of these c) .... have the majority.

6 The main objective of the ESCB is to ....

7 The NCBs fulfil all functions except ....

8 Interest rates are set by the ....

Text A

ORGANISATION OF THE EUROPEAN SYSTEM OF CENTRAL BANKS (ESCB)

The ESCB is composed of the European Central Bank (ECB) and the national central banks (NCBs) of the European Union member states.

In accordance with the ESCB Statute, the primary objective of the ESCB is to maintain price stability.

5 The basic tasks to be carried out by the ESCB are:

- to define and implement the monetary policy of the EU;
- to conduct foreign exchange operations;
- to hold and manage the official foreign reserves of the Member States; and
10 • to promote the smooth operation of payment systems.

In addition, the ESCB contributes to the smooth conduct of policies relating to supervision of credit institutions and the stability of the financial system. It also has an advisory role on matters which fall within its field of competence. Finally, in order to undertake the tasks of the ESCB, the ECB shall collect the necessary statistical information.

The European Central Bank, Frankfurt

From *www.ecb.int*

Text B

EUROPEAN CENTRAL BANK • by Wolfgang Münchau

Success of ECB critical for banking industry

The ECB is run by a six-member executive board headed by the ECB President and Vice-president. The four other members are in 5 charge of payment systems, banking supervision, international relations, organisation, statistics, banknotes and information systems.

10 The ECB took over from national central banks in setting interest rates from January 1999. Interest rates are now set by the ECB's governing council which 15 consists of the six-member executive board and the presidents of the national central banks of the participant countries.

The all-powerful council will 20 ensure the continued influence of national central banks in the decision-making process. The majority of the presidents of the NCBs versus the six ECB 'insiders' 25 will ensure that national interests will not be ignored under EMU[1].

Some critics have argued that this could give rise to a potentially destabilising situation. The ECB's 30 legal mandate is to pursue monetary policy with a view to the whole of the EMU area and without favouring one country over another. Yet if several 35 national central bank presidents were to form voting pacts, they could in theory outmanoeuvre the six executives.

Compared to the national 40 central banks, the ECB will be relatively small. While the Bank of France and the Bundesbank each employ more than 10,000 staff, the ECB will have to do with only 500 45 employees. The comparison is not entirely fair because the ECB's staff will be primarily engaged in research, security and payments systems, while most of the staff at 50 NCBs are involved in areas such as logistics and administration.

Because the national central banks will remain large and important, the transition to the 55 new regime will not mark a sudden shift. The Bundesbank will continue to exist and fulfil all its current functions except setting interest rates.

FINANCIAL TIMES
World business newspaper.

1 European Monetary Union

B Understanding details

Mark these sentences T (true) or F (false) according to the information in the texts.
Find the part of the text which gives the correct information.

1 The NCBs have no influence on the stability of the euro.   *F*

2 The ECB must consider the needs of all EMU countries equally.

3 The NCB presidents could overrule ECB decisions if they wanted to.

4 The staff of the Bundesbank is 20 times larger than that of the ECB.

5 ECB staff carry out the same tasks as NCB staff.

6 The creation of the ECB forced rapid changes to be made in Europe's central banking system.

Vocabulary tasks

A Word fields

Write these words and phrases in the appropriate columns.

> consist of   contribute to   give rise to   compared to   ensure   shift
> transition   be composed of   be run by   take over from   be in charge of
> be headed by   undertake   relatively small

organisational structure	responsibility	change	comparison
consist of	*contribute to*	*give rise to*	*compared to*
....	....	....	....
....	....	....	
....	....	....	

B Definitions

Match these terms with their definitions.

1 in accordance with	**a)** an obligation conferred by law
2 versus	**b)** to get an advantage by being more skilful than your opponents
3 legal mandate	**c)** in opposition to
4 voting pact	**d)** conforming to a law or regulation
5 outmanoeuvre	**e)** an agreement between several parties to vote in the same way for their own advantage

C Collocations

Match these verbs and nouns as they occur in the texts.

1	set	a)	monetary policy
2	fulfil	b)	foreign exchange operations
3	conduct	c)	foreign reserves
4	hold / manage	d)	interest rates
5	define / implement / pursue	e)	statistical information
6	collect	f)	price stability
7	maintain	g)	all functions

D Word families

Complete the chart.

verb	adjective	noun
supervise	supervisory	1 _supervision_
advise	2	advice
participate	3	4 ....
(de)stabilise	5	(de)stabilisation
influence	influential	6 ....

Over to you

1 Describe, orally or in writing, how the euro has performed recently.

2 Discuss these questions.
   a) Has European Monetary Union been a success or a failure?
   b) Has the ECB done a good job?
   c) Have there been any major disagreements between the ECB and the national central banks of the European member states?
   d) What do you think of the UK's position regarding the euro?
   e) Can you make any comparisons between the ECB and the US Federal Reserve?

3 Describe the structure of the organisation where you work or study.

Profitable banks

Before you read

Discuss these questions.

1 How do banks make their profits?

2 What factors determine the profitability of a bank?

Reading tasks

A Understanding main points

Mark these statements T (true) or F (false) according to the information in the text on the opposite page. Find the part of the text that gives the correct information.

1 Barclays' profits were higher than those of Lloyds TSB. *F*

2 Banks in the UK can make more profit by charging higher interest on loans. *F*

3 The provision for bad debts for the main UK banks was much higher in 1992. *T*

4 The banks do not employ as many clerks as they did in the 1980s. *T*

5 Customers prefer to deal with machines rather than talk to bank staff. *F*

6 British banks are the most advanced in the world. *F*

7 British banks face a lot of competition from other institutions offering financial services. *T*

8 The British don't complain very much about the service they receive from their banks. *F*

B Information search

Look quickly at the text and find the answers to these questions.

1 Which of the following reasons are given in the text to explain the British banks' profitability?

   a) trading in bond markets *✗*

   b) reduction in the number of branches *✓*

   c) effective management *✗*

   d) reduction in the level of bad debts *✗*

   e) interest from loans to overseas customers *✗*

   f) large-scale processing of transactions *✓*

   g) competitive interest rates attracting more customers *✓*

   h) British customers preferring to stay with the same bank *✓*

   i) the strength of the economy *✗*

Easy money

Britain's high street banks are extremely profitable – and widely criticised for their poor performance. What's going on? asks **George Graham**

Andrew Buxton, chairman of Barclays, ought to have looked a troubled man as he presented his 5 bank's annual results last week. In the last year, Barclays had lost a chief executive, dropped £205m on rash trading in the bond markets, another £153m on bad loans to 10 Russian customers, and had let its operating costs run out of control.

Yet Barclays somehow managed to make profits of £1.9bn.

In the same year, Lloyds TSB 15 reported a 14 per cent increase in its pre-tax profits to £3.29bn, equivalent to an after-tax return on shareholders' equity of 33 per cent. And other British banks 20 made similar profits.

So where do these profits come from? And why have they not been lost to the competition from other institutions?

25 The first part of the answer lies in the condition of the UK economy at large. In principle, bank profits are built for the most part on the volumes of loans they make 30 and the deposits they collect; the margins between the interest rates for these two sides of their balance sheet gives them their profits (or losses). But in a mature 35 market such as the UK, it is hard for a very large bank to expand loan and deposit volumes much beyond the level of the economy as a whole, and even harder to widen 40 net interest margins.

The biggest factor in bank profits has therefore been the level of bad debts. In 1992, when banks' accounts showed the worst of the 45 effects of the last UK recession, the seven principal banks set aside £6.45bn of bad debt provisions between them. Last year, the total for the same group is estimated to 50 have been around £2.6bn.

The other side of British banks' profitability reflects an interplay between technology-based efficiency gains and customer inertia.

55 Banks have become more efficient over the past decade, stripping out costs as new computer systems and telecommunications networks have enabled them to set 60 up industrial-scale processing plants for tasks that used to be handled by clerks in the back of each branch.

Branches are expensive to run, 65 and the network has been whittled down from a peak of 21,800 branches in 1985 to around 15,000 today. Each branch, too, has fewer staff.

70 One of the most frequent complaints is the disappearance of the human touch in the bank branch. Yet customers have reaped most of the benefits of the banks' efficiency 75 gains – cash dispensed at the touch of a button by machines, instant account balances, transfers and even loans available over the telephone.

80 However, British banks remain years behind their French rivals in electronic banking. Nor is the UK's money transmission system the most consumer-friendly in the 85 world. Customers in New Zealand and Canada get deposits credited instantaneously, while in the UK they must wait days.

Competition in financial services has been steadily increasing 90 since the 1980s. Yet the British consumer is more likely to swap a wife (or husband) than a bank. With such undemanding customers, leading banks could have years of fat profits ahead of them.

FINANCIAL TIMES
World business newspaper.

---

2 Which of the following examples of improved banking technology are mentioned either directly or indirectly in the text?

a) ATMs ✓

b) smart cards ✓

c) credit cards

d) telephone banking

e) electronic banking ✓

Vocabulary tasks

A Key terms

Match these terms with their definitions.

1 net interest margin

2 provisions

3 return on equity

4 money transmission system

a) money reserved to cover bad debts

b) profit as a percentage of shareholders' capital

c) difference between interest income and interest payments

d) method of transferring funds from one person to another

B Word search

Replace the underlined items with words or phrases from the text that have a similar meaning.

1 Banks are affected by the state of the UK economy in general. (para 5) *at large*

2 The UK has a very established loan market. (para 5)

3 It's difficult for a large bank to increase loan and deposit volumes. (para 5)

4 The UK's seven principal banks set aside about £6.5bn of bad debt provision. (para 6)

5 Banks have closed thousands of branches over the last ten years. (para 8)

6 Many routine banking tasks are dealt with by computer. (para 8)

7 A bank branch is expensive to operate. (para 9)

8 Technologically, British banks are behind their French competitors. (para 11)

9 Few people change banks in Britain. (para 12)

10 Most UK banks still make huge profits. (para 12)

C Understanding expressions

Choose the best explanation for each of these words or phrases from the text.

1 troubled (line 3)
   a) worried ✓
   b) pleased

2 rash trading (line 8)
   a) trading without enough care and consideration. ✓
   b) trading in large volumes

3 let its operating costs run out of control (line 10)
   a) allowed its costs to go over the budget ✓
   b) allowed its costs to be checked by external auditors

4 customer inertia (line 54)
   a) customers don't want to move or change anything ✓
   b) customers expect a lot of improvements in service

5 stripping out costs (line 56)
   a) adding to costs
   b) removing costs

6 reaped most of the benefits (line 73)
   a) collected most of the benefits
   b) lost most of the benefits

D Word search

Find a word or phrase in the text that has a similar meaning.

1 total amounts or quantities (para 5)

volumes ....

2 system of local offices spread around the country (para 9)

b................... n...................

3 highest level recorded over a period (para 9)

p...................

4 designed so as to be of maximum benefit to the consumer (para 11)

c...................-f...................

5 when the value of a deposit is added to an account balance (para 11)

c...................

6 banks with the biggest share of the market (para 12)

l................... b...................

E Linking

Match the first half of each sentence with the most appropriate second half. Notice the words that are used in each sentence to mark a contrasting idea. (These words are in italics.)

1 Barclays Bank had a troubled year
2 Banks make a profit on their net interest margin
3 British banks have introduced a range of technically-advanced services
4 Canadian customers get deposits credited instantaneously

a) *while* UK customers have to wait a few days.
b) *yet* it managed to make a lot of profit.
c) *but* it is difficult for them to widen their margins.
d) *but* they are still behind the French in electronic banking.

Over to you

1 If possible, find the annual results of a bank in your country and report on its profitability.

2 How do British banks differ from banks in your country in the way they make their profits?

Bank mergers

Before you read

1 Answer these questions.

   a) Which is the correct description of a merger?
   When one company gains control of another by buying the majority of its shares.
   When two companies, often equal in size, combine to form one new company.

   b) What word or words fit the other description above?

2 Discuss these questions.

   a) What kinds of banks and financial institutions are there in your country?

   b) Is there a trend in your country for smaller banks to merge or be taken over by larger ones?

Reading tasks

A Understanding main points

1 Mark these statements T (true) or F (false) according to the information in the text on the opposite page. Find the part of the text that gives the correct information.

   a) In investment banking, it is important to be very big in order to be competitive. *T*

   b) Middle-sized banks may survive, but small ones have no chance.

   c) Barclays, a UK bank, has increased its investment banking activities.

   d) It is difficult for middle-sized banks to pay the high salaries demanded by stock traders.

   e) Edward Crutchfield's comments were about retail banking.

   f) Mergers between retail banks are mostly international.

   g) There are more financial institutions in relation to the population in France than in the USA.

   h) Irish banks need to become international if they want to expand.

   i) In retail banking it is difficult to save costs by increasing size.

   j) Credit card processing is cheaper when done on a large scale.

   k) One of the biggest costs for banks nowadays is software development.

2 The article can be divided into two sections, each dealing with a different aspect. These are marked I and II in the text. What is each section about?

3 Find three kinds of bank which are mentioned in the article.

FINANCIAL TIMES   TUESDAY JANUARY 13 1998   ★★

BANKING • by George Graham

Survival of the biggest

A wave of M&A has reshaped the industry, but stuck largely to national deals

How big is big? A wave of mergers and acquisitions has completely reshaped the face of the international finance industry. Across a range of financial sectors, the tables are being cleared for a handful of giants, with room still for niche players but little space for the middle-sized.

I The most dramatic changes came in the investment banking area, where a range of specialised or regional investment banks found new commercial banking parents. Many investment bankers now believe the battle for membership of dominant firms is reaching its closing stages.

'In a lot of industries – telecoms, pharmaceuticals, for example – it is not unusual to see five global giants survive. Five seems to be the magic number,' says Hans de Gier, head of Warburg Dillon Read investment bank. 'In investment banking, too, you will see a handful of global firms which have the cost base but also have the revenue base to support this vision.'

Some banks have already reached the conclusion that they cannot realistically hope to be part of that select group, and have scaled back their investment banking ambitions. In the UK, both Barclays and National Westminster have sold most of their equity operations and now concentrate solely on debt – more closely linked to their traditional banking business.

Spiralling pay packets for traders and investment bankers have made it difficult for the mid-sized contenders to stay in the race. They have to pay people just as much or more, but don't get as much revenue out of them as a global firm.

II In the retail banking sector, some of the talk sounds familiar. Edward Crutchfield, chairman of First Union, recently warned smaller traditional banks that they were a 'declining, dying business. Merger mania will last until there are 10 or 12 or maybe 15 dominant financial services.'

But with very few exceptions, consolidation in the retail banking sector remains national in character. ING's takeover of Banque Bruxelles Lambert in Belgium represents one example of a cross-border deal. But most efforts to cross national boundaries have not worked.

In the US, there remains plenty of room for consolidation without stretching overseas. The number of commercial banks has shrunk from 11,462 in 1992 to 9,215 this year, but that still leaves the US with far more financial institutions in proportion to its population than comparable countries.

In countries such as the UK and France there may be room for further consolidation, but banks in the Netherlands and Ireland already have to look abroad for a second home market.

Retail banking has proved resistant to economies of scale. In specific activities such as credit card processing, unit costs fall rapidly with size. In banking more generally, however, the complexity of operations reduces the benefits resulting from size.

That may be changing with increasing IT[1] use in banking. The cost of software development is one of the biggest factors with 14 banks estimated to be spending more than $1 billion a year on IT.

FINANCIAL TIMES
World business newspaper.

i Information Technology

Vocabulary tasks

A Match these terms with their definitions.

1 consolidation
2 equity operations
3 unit cost
4 cost base
5 niche
6 parent company
7 retail banking
8 investment bank
9 commercial bank

a) division of a bank that deals with share issues and share trading
b) bank that acts as an intermediary between companies and the investing public
c) bringing together of two or more companies, as in a merger
d) provision of basic banking services to individuals and companies
e) place in the market for a specialised product or service
f) company which owns more than 50% of another company
g) total cost divided by the number of items that are handled
h) large size providing the means for costs to be minimised
i) bank involved in international trade and corporate banking

B Word search

Find a word or phrase in the text that has similar meaning.

1 people or companies who compete to win something (para 5)
c*ontenders*.....

2 temporary phase when everybody wants to merge (para 6)
m................... m...................

3 merger or takeover between companies in different countries (para 7)
c...................-b................... d...................

4 principle that the larger a company is, the lower its average costs are (para 10)
e................... of s...................

C Word fields

Write these words or phrases in the appropriate columns.

| expand   reduce   scale back   shrink   stretch   spiral   decline   fall |

Words meaning to get bigger
...............*expand*.....................

Words meaning to get smaller
...............*reduce*.....................

D Understanding expressions

Choose the best explanation for each of these words or phrases from the text.

1 wave of mergers (line 1)
   a) large number of mergers taking place all at once   ✓
   b) tendency for a few mergers to take place

2 reshaped the face of the international financial industry (line 3)
   a) changed it completely
   b) improved it

3 tables are being cleared (line 6)
   a) new game is about to start with different players taking part
   b) the game is over

4 reaching its closing stages (line 18)
   a) has finished
   b) nearly at an end

5 handful (line 27)
   a) five
   b) small number

6 vision (line 30)
   a) view of the future
   b) plan or policy

7 concentrate solely on (line 40)
   a) concentrate mainly on
   b) concentrate only on

8 comparable countries (line 77)
   a) countries that are similar in size
   b) countries that have a similar level of economic development

9 has proved resistant to (line 85)
   a) has benefited from
   b) has been unaffected by

10 unit costs fall rapidly with size (line 88)
   a) unit costs fall rapidly as size increases
   b) unit costs fall rapidly as size decreases

Over to you

1 Discuss what changes have taken place since 1997 regarding the shape of the financial industry.

2 What do you think the financial industry will look like in ten years' time? Will there be many more changes? Give your opinion.

Currency markets

Before you read

1 Discuss this question.

What kinds of events can cause currencies to fluctuate?

2 Answer these questions.

   a) What words do you know that describe a *rise* or *increase* in currency value? Make a list.

   b) Make another list of words that describe a *fall* or *decrease*.

   c) The words below are used in the texts on the opposite page. Add them to one of your lists according to whether they indicate a *rise* or a *fall*.

shoot up ↗   regain   move lower   drop   weaken   boost   decline   slide   gain

Reading tasks

A Understanding main points

Mark these statements T (true) or F (false) according to the information in the texts on the opposite page. Find the part of the text that gives the correct information.

  1 The dollar rose against both the euro and the yen on January 8th.   *F*

  2 Figures that showed the strength of the US economy were published on January 8th.

  3 During trading on January 8th, the dollar increased rapidly but then fell slightly.

  4 The yen has been at a high level because of Japanese monetary policy.

  5 The US Ambassador to Japan said it was true that he had pressed Japan to change its policy.

  6 The yen fell against the dollar on February 10th, but it rose again later.

  7 The dollar fell against the euro on March 8th.

  8 Before March 8th, the euro had increased against the dollar.

  9 Currency analysts gave the opinion that the euro would continue to get stronger.

 10 Jane Foley thinks that the ECB will intervene to prevent the euro from falling any further.

B Information search

Which of the following are given as causes of currency fluctuations in the three texts?

  1 unemployment figures ✓

  2 stock market increases

  3 trade deficit

  4 rumours of capital flows

  5 trade surplus

  6 retail sales figures

  7 forecasts of economic growth

  8 changes in government policy

  9 intervention by the central bank

A

FINANCIAL TIMES   SATURDAY JANUARY 9 1999   ★★

Dollar's boost

MARKETS REPORT

**By Alan Beattie
and Melanie Carroll**

The dollar shot up against the euro on the back of employment data showing the US economy continuing to surge ahead.

5   Traders struggled to recall the last time that a piece of data rather than rumours of capital flows had moved the dollar, a tentative sign some degree of normal- 10 ity was returning to the markets.

After rising nearly a cent in a few minutes after the data were released in the middle of the European session, the dollar con- 15 solidated its new position. At the end of London trading it closed at $1.155 against the euro, up from $1.167 the previous day.

But against the yen, the dollar 20 remained unmoved by the data, evidence that many traders expect the dollar's next move to be further down against the Japanese currency.

25   In late afternoon in New York the dollar was trading at 1.1605 to the euro and 110.90 to the yen.

FINANCIAL TIMES
World business newspaper.

B

FINANCIAL TIMES   THURSDAY FEBRUARY 11 1999   ★★

Yen drops on reports of US pressure

MARKETS REPORT

**By Alan Beattie
and Melanie Carroll**

Rumours that the US administration was actively pushing Japan to loosen monetary policy knocked the yen sharply lower against the 5 dollar yesterday.

Reports in the US press claimed that Washington was pressing the Bank of Japan to ease monetary policy, weakening the yen.

10   Despite a denial of this by Thomas Foley, the US ambassador to Japan, the yen dropped sharply lower against the dollar during the Asian trading session. It regained 15 some of those losses in London trading hours, closing at ¥114.5, slightly lower than its close of ¥114.4 on Tuesday.

The yen also fell against the euro, closing down at ¥129.7.

FINANCIAL TIMES
World business newspaper.

C

FINANCIAL TIMES   TUESDAY MARCH 9 1999   ★★

Tietmeyer sparks euro profit taking

MARKETS REPORT

**By Alan Beattie
and Melanie Carroll**

The euro gained against the dollar yesterday after Hans Tietmeyer, president of the Bundesbank, said he did not want to see the euro 5 continue its present slide.

Mr Tietmeyer's comments gave the currency a rare boost, with traders looking to take profits on long dollar positions.

10   The euro gained nearly a cent yesterday from its low point of $1.08 on March 5th, closing in London at $1.088.

But analysts said that the relief 15 for the currency might be short-lived. Jane Foley, currency analyst at Barclays Capital in London, said the euro's gains were a natural response to recent lows, and in 20 her view it would remain weak in the medium term.

She expected the euro–dollar rate to react to key German unemployment data to be released 25 today, and to the US retail sales figures due on Thursday.

'I don't think the pace of decline at the moment is significant. And I don't think the ECB[1] is worried 30 about the euro's downside yet, although if it moves sharply lower the ECB will probably move in to calm things down,' she said.

FINANCIAL TIMES
World business newspaper.

1 European Central Bank

C Understanding details

1 Mark three values for the euro against the dollar in Graph 1 for the dates 8 January, 5 March and 8 March 1999.

2 Mark three values for the yen against the dollar in Graph 2 for the dates 8 January, and 9–10 February 1999.

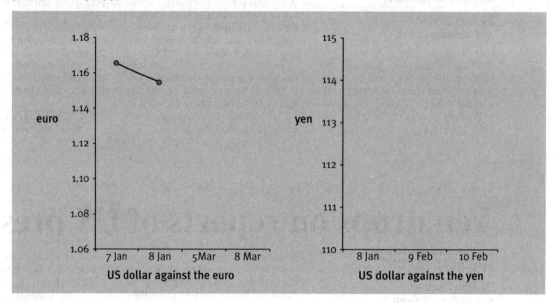

Vocabulary tasks

A Word search

Find a word or phrase in the texts that has a similar meaning.

1 unofficial talk or opinion not always based on fact (Text A, para 2)

r*umours*........

2 movement of large amounts of money (Text A, para 2)

c................... f...................

3 dollar rate agreed in advance for deals in six months' or one year's time (Text C, para 2)

l.................. d................... p...................

4 minimum level recorded during a specified period (Text C, para 3)

l.................. p...................

5 statistics showing consumer spending in the country as a whole (Text C, para 5)

r................... s................... f...................

B Word search

Replace the underlined items with words and phrases from the texts that have a similar meaning.

1 The dollar <u>increased rapidly</u> against the euro. (Text A, para 1) *shot up*

2 Employment <u>figures</u> showed that the US economy was getting stronger. (Text A, para 1)

3 The figures were <u>made public</u> in the middle of the European session. (Text A, para 3)

4 Reports in the US <u>newspapers</u> said that the yen should weaken. (Text B, para 2)

5 Jane Foley doesn't think the speed of decline in the euro is <u>big</u> enough to worry about. (Text C, para 6)

C Understanding expressions

Choose the best explanation for each of these words or phrases from the texts.

1 on the back of employment data (Text A, line 2)
   a) as a result of employment data being published ✓
   b) because employment data was unavailable

2 surge ahead (Text A, line 4)
   a) grow more rapidly than other economies
   b) decline more rapidly than other economies

3 tentative sign (Text A, line 8)
   a) strong sign
   b) gentle sign

4 consolidated its new position (Text A, line 14)
   a) became steady after some fluctuations
   b) continued to grow

5 loosen monetary policy (Text B, line 3)
   a) slightly reduce control of the economy
   b) greatly reduce control of the economy

6 knocked the yen lower (Text B, line 3)
   a) had a slight impact on the yen, making it fall
   b) had a strong impact on the yen, making it fall

7 looking to take profits (Text C, line 8)
   a) hoping to take profits
   b) seeing other people take profits

Over to you

1 Find some recent figures comparing the movements of two currencies. Draw a graph to show these movements and then describe it.

2 Explain the reasons for recent increases or falls in your own currency.

Sending money overseas: priority payments

Discuss these questions.

1 What do you think a priority payment is?
2 If you have to send money quickly to a person in another country, what do you normally do?
3 How long does the payment take to arrive?
4 What kind of problems could you have when making overseas payments?

A Understanding main points

Read the text on the opposite page about sending money overseas and match the questions below (1–6) with paragraphs in the text (a–f).

1 Is it possible to guarantee a payment date? *paragraph d*
2 When will my account be debited and how will I be informed?
3 What charges will I have to pay?
4 When should I use this type of payment?
5 Is it possible to cancel a payment instruction?
6 How long will it take for the beneficiary to receive the funds?

B Understanding details

Mark these statements T (true) or F (false) according to the information in the text. Find the part of the text that gives the correct information.

1 Priority payments cost more than other kinds of payments. *T*
2 Priority payments should only be used to send money to developed countries.
3 The exchange rate for foreign currency payments is always determined by the International Banking Centre.
4 It is not possible for the bank to guarantee a payment date.
5 It is not a problem to change your mind about a payment after the money has been sent.
6 The person who makes the payment normally has to pay the overseas bank charges.

How To Send Money Overseas From The United Kingdom

Priority Payments

● **a)** ....

Priority payments are the fastest and most secure method of making an international payment. Consequently they are slightly more expensive than other payment methods. This type of payment should be used when speed of delivery is the most important factor. We also recommend this type of payment to the less well-developed countries of the world. Payments are sent by SWIFT, which is an electronic payment system, to any country in the world in sterling or any tradable foreign currency. If you instruct us to make a foreign currency payment we will use the prevailing exchange rate published in your branch on a daily basis. For high value payments we will obtain a rate for you from our International Banking Centre. We instruct a bank in the receiving country to inform the beneficiary, i.e. the recipient of the payment, that you have sent some money and:

- credit a specified bank account, or –
- pay the beneficiary at a specified address, or –
- hold funds for the beneficiary to collect upon production of a passport or other means of identification.

● **b)** ....

The beneficiary should normally receive funds within three or four working days from the instruction leaving your branch. This timescale is dependent upon how much information you can provide regarding the beneficiary's banking arrangements and whether HSBC is in direct account relationship[1] with the beneficiary's bankers. In urgent cases these times can be improved upon if payment instructions are telephoned by your branch to the local International Banking Centre.

● **c)** ....

Your account will be debited on the day HSBC sends your payment overseas. A debit advice will be sent to you by your branch within three working days.

● **d)** ....

The value date, i.e. payment date, is the date on which funds should be available to the beneficiary's bank to make payment to the beneficiary. HSBC can achieve same-day value in a few financial centres. Otherwise customers can expect payments to be made within three or four working days. Value may, however, be delayed if there are complications in the routing of payments or in overseas banking systems. AS A RESULT WE CAN GIVE NO GENERAL ASSURANCES ON THE ACHIEVEMENT OF VALUE DATES. YOU ARE THEREFORE ENCOURAGED TO DISCUSS YOUR NEEDS WITH BRANCH STAFF: THEY ARE THERE TO HELP YOU.

● **e)** ....

Once we have transmitted funds overseas it is almost impossible to cancel the instruction. Depending on the circumstances, HSBC will agree to such a request and will endeavour to retrieve funds. If we are successful in obtaining a refund, your account will be credited after deducting any expenses, which can be substantial.

● **f)** ....

HSBC's standard tariff is quoted in our booklet, 'International Tariff for Personal Customers' and can be paid by either yourself or the beneficiary. When HSBC transfers money overseas, the receiving bank may deduct charges from the payment before crediting the beneficiary. It is possible for you to pay the overseas bank's charge, thus ensuring the beneficiary receives the gross amount of the payment. However, you should be aware that some countries charge a percentage tariff with no maximum. Therefore if you were sending a high value payment it is possible that you could incur substantial overseas charges.

---

1 The bank has an account at the foreign bank where the payment is going.

From *A guide to making international payments through Midland,* HSBC publications

Vocabulary tasks

A Word search

Find a word or phrase in the text that has a similar meaning.

1 person who receives or will receive a payment (para a)

b *eneficiary*.....

2 confirmation that money has been deducted from your account (para c)

d.................. a...................

3 day on which funds reach the beneficiary's bank (para d)

v.................. d...................

4 money returned to a person who wishes to cancel a payment (para e)

r...................

5 schedule of prices or fees (para f)

t..................

B Synonyms

Which words or phrases have similar meanings? Match them.

1	advice	a)	transmit
2	prevailing	b)	recover
3	retrieve	c)	charge
4	quote	d)	debit
5	send	e)	notice
6	deduct	f)	current
7	tariff	g)	payment date
8	value date	h)	publish

C Word families

Write the correct form of the word in brackets in each sentence.

1 (receive) The beneficiary is the ...*recipient*.... of a payment.

2 (produce) The beneficiary can only collect the money upon .... of some identification.

3 (advise) After making the payment, your bank sends you an .... that your account has been debited.

4 (deliver) A priority payment is made when the speed of .... is important.

5 (day) The exchange rate is published on a .... basis.

D Collocations

Match these verbs and nouns as they occur in the text.

1 make   **a)** an account
2 incur   **b)** a tariff
3 credit   **c)** a date
4 charge   **d)** a payment
5 guarantee   **e)** an assurance
6 give   **f)** charges

E Linking

Match the statements. Notice the words used to link the ideas (in italics).

1 Overseas banking systems can be complex.

2 Some overseas banks charge a percentage tariff with no maximum,

3 It is difficult to cancel a payment instruction.

4 It is possible for the sender to pay the overseas bank charges,

5 Priority payments are sent by an electronic payment system.

6 Instructions can be telephoned directly to the International Banking Centre,

a) *However*, HSBC will try to retrieve funds in some situations.

b) *Consequently* payments are sometimes delayed.

c) *As a result*, they are faster than other payment methods.

d) *therefore* charges can be very high.

e) *thus* improving the payment time.

f) *otherwise* it is normally the beneficiary who pays.

Over to you

1 Imagine you are an HSBC banking officer. Explain, to a potential customer, how the priority payment method works.

2 Explain another payment method used by banks in your country.

3 Imagine you are a bank customer. Make a list of questions you would like to ask about priority payments. Write a letter to HSBC asking them to answer these questions.

12 Foreign trade

Before you read

Discuss these questions.

1 What are some of the risks involved in trading internationally?

2 What payment methods do you know that are used when exporting or importing goods?

3 What is the role of the banks in international trade?

Reading tasks

A Understanding main points

Read the text on the opposite page about payment methods for exporters and write the four methods in the correct positions according to their risks for the exporter.

Least secure   Payment method: 1 .... *open account* ....

2 ....

3 ....

Most secure   4 ....

B Understanding details

Mark these statements T (true) or F (false) according to the information in the text. Find the part of the text that gives the correct information.

Open account

1 The importer pays for the goods after receiving the documents.   T

2 There is no contract involved.

3 The exporter must be able to trust the buyer.

Documentary credit

4 If a letter of credit is issued, the importer's bank agrees to pay for the goods without conditions.

5 If a letter of credit is confirmed, the exporter's bank takes responsibility for payment.

Bills for collection

6 Commercial documents and the document of title are always enclosed with a bill of exchange.

7 Importers may not accept the bill of exchange until the goods arrive.

8 Exporters can keep control of goods by sending bills of lading through the banking system.

9 Exporters reduce risk if documents are released against acceptance of the bill rather than payment.

Advance payment

10 This means that the importer has to pay before any goods are dispatched.

• Open Account

The goods, and relevant documents, are sent by the exporter directly to the overseas buyer, who will have agreed to remit payment of the invoice back to the exporter upon arrival of the documents or within a certain period after the invoice date. The exporter loses all control of the goods, trusting that
5   payment will be made by the importer in accordance with the original sales contract.

• Documentary Credit

Documentary Credit is often referred to as a Letter of Credit. This is an undertaking issued by an overseas bank to a UK exporter through a bank in the UK, to pay for the goods provided that the exporter complies fully with the conditions established by the Documentary Credit.

10   Additional security can be obtained by obtaining the 'confirmation' of a UK bank[1] to the transaction, thereby transferring the responsibility from the importer's bank overseas to a more familiar bank in the country of the exporter.

Very few risks arise for the exporter because the potential problem areas of the buyer risk and country risk can be eliminated. However, the exporter must present the correct documents and comply fully
15   with the terms and conditions of the credit. Failure to do so could result in the exporter losing the protection of the credit.

• Bills for Collection

Trade collections are initiated when an exporter draws a bill of exchange on an overseas buyer. This is forwarded by the exporter's bank in the importer's country.

20   Such collections may be either 'documentary' or 'clean'[2]. A documentary collection is one in which the commercial documents and, if appropriate, the documents of title to the goods are enclosed with the bill of exchange. These are sent by the exporter's bank to a bank in the importer's country together with instructions to release the documentation against either payment or acceptance of the bill.

The risks that the exporter has to face are that the importer fails to accept the bill of exchange or
25   dishonours an accepted bill[3] upon maturity. This means that the exporter may have to consider shipping the goods back to the UK, finding an alternative buyer or even abandoning the consignment, all of which could be expensive.

In many areas of the world it is common practice to defer presentation[4], payment or acceptance until arrival of the carrying vessel. Collection and remittance charges can also be relatively high.

30   If the exporter retains control over the goods by remitting a full set of Bills of Lading[5] through the intermediary of the banking system, control of the goods will be handed over to the importer only against payment or acceptance of the bill by the importer. If the documents are released against the importer's acceptance of the bill, control of the goods is lost and the accepted bill of exchange may be dishonoured at maturity.

35 ### • Advance Payment

Exporters receive payment from an overseas buyer in full, or in part, before the goods are dispatched. This means that the exporter has no risks associated with non-payment.

From *Guide for exporting and importing*, HSBC publications

---

1 This bank is then known as the confirming bank.
2 Clean means that no documents are involved.
3 The importer does not pay, although he had previously agreed to pay.
4 This means to delay passing the bill to the importer.
5 This means sending all the necessary shipping documents.

C Information search

Match the risks (**a–g**) with the payment methods.

1 Open account
2 Documentary credit
3 Bills for collection
4 Advance payment

a) Exporters must comply with the conditions of the credit documents.
b) Importers may delay payment.
c) Importers may not pay at all.
d) It takes a long time to process payment in some countries.
e) Importers may not accept the bill of exchange.
f) Bank charges may be high.
g) Exporters must take care to present the correct documents.

Vocabulary tasks

A Key terms

Match these terms with their definitions.

1 invoice
2 clean collection
3 documentary collection
4 bill of exchange
5 bill of lading
6 document of title
7 issuing bank
8 collecting bank
9 confirming bank
10 letter of credit

a) document that shows details of goods being transported; it entitles the receiver to collect the goods on arrival
b) list of goods sold as a request for payment
c) bank that issues a letter of credit (i.e. the importer's bank)
d) bank that receives payment of bills, etc. for their customer's account (i.e. the exporter's bank)
e) document allowing someone to claim ownership of goods
f) payment by bill of exchange to which documents are not attached
g) signed document that orders a person or organisation to pay a fixed sum of money on demand or on a specified date
h) bank that confirms they will pay the exporter on evidence of shipment of goods
i) method of financing overseas trade where payment is made by a bank in return for delivery of commercial documents, provided that the terms and conditions of the contract are met
j) payment by bill of exchange to which commercial documents (and sometimes a document of title) are attached

B Word search

Find a word or phrase in the text that has a similar meaning.

1 promise or guarantee given to or by a bank (para 2)

u...................

2 load of goods sent to a customers (para 7)

c...................

3 person or company that acts as a middleman in a transaction (para 9)

i...................

4 date when a bill of exchange is due for payment (para 9)

m...................

C Complete the sentence

Use an appropriate form of the words in the box to complete the sentences which describe the procedure for documentary collection.

draw   accept   dishonour   release   remit   forward   dispatch   present

1 The first step the exporter takes is to ask his bank to ...*draw*......... a bill of exchange on the overseas buyer.

2 The exporter's bank .... the bill of exchange, together with the commercial documents, to the importer's bank.

3 At the same time, the exporter .... the goods.

4 The exporter must take care to .... the correct documents to the bank.

5 When the importer .... the bill of exchange, the bank will .... the documents of title to the goods.

6 If the importer .... the bill, the exporter may have to find an alternative buyer or ship the goods back again.

7 In some parts of the world, banks may be slow to .... payment to the exporter's bank.

Over to you

1 The text in this unit describes the risks of each payment method from the exporter's point of view. What are the risks for the importer? Which methods will be secure and why?

2 Imagine you are a banker talking to one of your customers who has never exported before. Explain how documentary credit works.

3 Prepare a list of recommendations for either exporters or importers.

Economic reports

1 Discuss these questions.

a) When you assess the strength of a nation's economy, what factors do you normally consider?

b) If a nation has severe economic difficulties, what can it do?

2 Match the terms below with their definitions.

1 trade surplus	**a)**	payment of interest on a debt
2 trade deficit	**b)**	reduction in the exchange value of a country's currency
3 treasury bills	**c)**	instruments of government borrowing
4 debt service	**d)**	value of a country's exports exceeds the value of its imports
5 devaluation	**e)**	value of a country's imports exceeds the value of its exports

Reading tasks

A Information search

Look quickly at the three texts on the opposite page and answer these questions.

1 Which country has a problem paying the interest on its foreign debts?   *Ukraine*

2 In which country is the trade surplus decreasing?

3 Which country has recently devalued its currency?

4 Which country is trying to keep inflation down?

5 Which country is hoping to increase its exports by 4%?

B Understanding main points

Mark these statements T (true) or F (false) according to the information in the texts. Find the part of the text that gives the correct information.

1 The Brazilian economy is in recession because of its high interest rates.   *T*

2 GDP in Brazil has been falling for the past six months.

3 The Brazilian economy has been in decline since 1992.

4 It is predicted that Brazilian exports will decrease.

5 The IMF has, for the present, discontinued payments to the Ukraine.

6 The Ukraine did not meet all of the terms of the IMF credit.

7 The Ukraine government has only foreign debts.

8 The gap between Thailand's imports and exports is increasing.

9 The decline in Thailand's imports is slowing down.

10 Economists are unhappy about Thailand's import figures.

Text A

Brazil's high rates bring recession

By Geoff Dyer in São Paulo

Brazil formally moved into recession at the end of last year as the high interest rate policy aimed at preventing a
5 currency crisis caused the economy to show its worst annual record of economic growth since 1992.

Gross domestic product fell
10 1.89 per cent in the fourth quarter compared with the same period the year before, the second consecutive quarter of negative growth.
15 As a result, the economy grew by just 0.15% last year, the worst result since the 0.54 per cent decline in 1992 and down from the 3.68 per cent
20 growth of the year before.

Interest rates were kept high throughout the fourth quarter. However, the government was forced to let the
25 currency float in January, causing an immediate devaluation of 38% against the dollar. With interest rates currently 39%, monetary pol-
30 icy is now being kept tight to reduce the inflationary impact of the devaluation.

Economists are predicting a fall this year of between 3
35 and 6 per cent in GDP, although some believe the economy could start growing by the end of the year.

The government is fore-
40 casting a trade surplus this year of $6–$7bn, compared to a deficit of $6.4bn last year.

FINANCIAL TIMES
World business newspaper.

Text B

UKRAINE'S EXTERNAL DEBT SERVICING

Worries over IMF loan delay

Ukraine may be forced to renegotiate part of its external debt service if a loan from the International Monetary Fund continues to be delayed past March, said Ihor Mitiukov, Ukraine's finance minister.
5   He said he was confident the Ukrainian government and the IMF would agree on continued payment of the loan next month, which has been held up since November because of Ukraine's failure to meet a number of conditions of the $2.2bn three-year credit granted by the IMF last August.
10   But, if continued payments could not be agreed on, 'we will be simply forced to begin negotiations with our external creditors,' he said.

The Ukrainian government owes $1.9bn in external debt service this year, together with 1.5bn hryvnia in payments on domestic treasury bills.

FINANCIAL TIMES
World business newspaper.

Text C

THAILAND ECONOMY

Trade surplus narrows

Thailand's trade surplus narrowed in January, a sign that exports – a key component of the economy – may revive in the coming months. The trade surplus in January was $816m compared with a surplus in December of $1.23bn.
5 Exports fell 4.8 per cent compared with an 8.5 per cent decline a month earlier. Imports were also down 4.8 per cent year-on-year compared with a decline of 15.8 per cent in the previous month.

Economists say the bottoming-out of the crucial import
10 figure – this is the first single-digit decline in more than a year – offers hope for exports later this year as Thailand's exportable goods traditionally have a high import content. The central bank forecasts 4 per cent growth in exports this year. Imports must pick up and the trade deficit must narrow for that target to be reached.

FINANCIAL TIMES
World business newspaper.

Vocabulary tasks

A Key terms

Match the expressions with the graphs that illustrate them. (More than one expression can be matched to some graphs.)

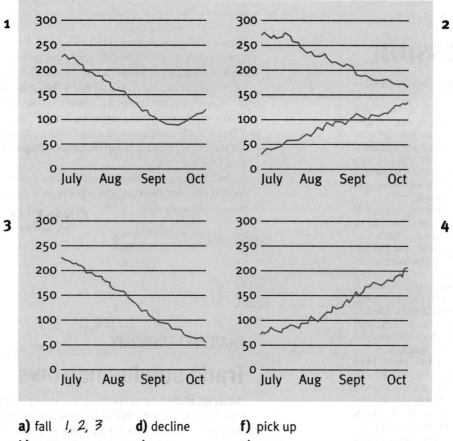

a) fall *1, 2, 3*   d) decline   f) pick up

b) grow   e) revive   g) narrow

c) bottom out

B Word search

Find a word or phrase in the texts that has a similar meaning.

1 recession (Text A, para 2)

   n.................. g..................

2 forecasting (Text A, para 5)

   p..................

3 loan (Text B, para 2)

   c..................

4 held up (Text B, para 1)

   d..................

C Understanding expressions

Choose the best explanation for each of these phrases from the text.

1 let the currency float (Text A, line 24)
   a) allow the currency to find its true level ✓
   b) try to keep the currency at a specified level against another currency

2 monetary policy is being kept tight (Text A, line 29)
   a) the government is implementing strict controls on the economy
   b) the government is controlling the economy but not very strongly

3 be forced to (Text B, line 1)
   a) have to do something because there is no alternative
   b) get an advantage from doing something

4 single-digit decline (Text C, line 10)
   a) a fall of less than 10%
   b) a fall of greater than 10%

5 Thailand's exportable goods have a high import content (Text C, line 11)
   a) a high level of imports means competition for Thai products
   b) Thailand needs to import a lot of raw materials for manufacturing export goods

D Word search

Replace the underlined items with words or phrases from the texts that have a similar meaning.

1 The Brazilian government has a plan of action to reduce inflation. (Text A, para 1) *policy*

2 Brazil's economy is in a state of extreme danger. (Text A, para 1)

3 GDP fell over two quarters, one immediately following the other. (Text A, para 2)

4 Ukraine will have problems paying interest to the people it owes money to. (Text B, para 3)

5 Exports are an important part of the economy. (Text C, para 1)

6 The trade surplus was $816m, whereas it was $1.2bn last year. (Text C, para 1)

E Complete the sentence

Use an appropriate verb from the texts to complete each sentence.

1 When you negotiate, you try to ....*agree*........ on terms.

2 It will be difficult to .... the target of 4% growth next year.

3 The IMF .... credit to the Ukraine for a three-year period.

4 The government was unable to .... the conditions that had been agreed.

Over to you

1 Describe the state of the economy in your country. If possible, find some recent economic figures in the form of charts or graphs and describe them.

2 Write a short report on the economy of your own country, or of another country that you know well.

14 Project finance

Before you read

1 Discuss these questions.

a) How are large projects, such as the construction of roads or bridges, usually financed?

b) What role does the World Bank play in project financing?

2 Match these terms with their definitions.

1 consortium	**a)** short-term loan made by banks to cover the time between when money is first needed and when other funding becomes available
2 syndicated loan	**b)** combination of two or more large international companies, formed for a special purpose for a limited period
3 bridging finance	
4 government subsidies	**c)** bank which strengthens developing economies by supporting large projects such as infrastructure projects
5 development bank	**d)** money provided from the nation's current account to enable a company (or other recipient) to operate without loss
6 LIBOR	**e)** loan arranged for a large organisation or government by a lead bank with other banks participating
	f) rate of interest at which funds are offered on loan on the interbank market, which may be used as the bank's base rate

Reading tasks

A Understanding main points

Mark these statements T (true) or F (false) according to the information in the texts on the opposite page. Find the part of the text that gives the correct information.

Uganda hydroelectric deal

1 If AES builds the new dam at Bujagali Falls, the country's power supply will increase to 250MW.   *F*

2 Currently, economic growth in Uganda is restricted by inadequate power supplies.

3 Foreign investors are worried about Uganda going to war with its neighbours.

4 Norpak Power is a company which favours a Norwegian Hydroelectric scheme.

5 The Norwegian project would be smaller and less expensive than the American one.

6 It is expected that both projects will go ahead.

Croatian motorways

7 The bridging loan for this project will amount to €68.8m.

8 Construction of the new motorway cannot start until financing for the whole project has been found.

9 Domestic banks are leading the consortium that will provide bridging finance.

10 The rate for the syndicated loan is above the London Interbank rate.

11 There have been problems persuading banks to lend to central Europe in the past.

Text A

POWER DEVELOPMENT RIVAL SCHEMES PUT FORWARD TO END CHRONIC ELECTRICITY SHORTAGES

Uganda 'close to big hydroelectric deal'

By Mark Turner in Nairobi

AES, the US independent power company, says it is about to sign a deal to construct a $500m 250MW[1] hydroelectric dam at Uganda's Bujagali Falls, a project that would double the country's power supply.

The investment – East Africa's biggest – would show confidence in Uganda, at a time of concern at corruption and the potential cost of the military involvement in the Democratic Republic of Congo.

Uganda suffers from severe power shortages, which a recent World Bank study cited as a major impediment to investment. The government estimates that shortages reduce GDP growth by 2 per cent a year.

The country's current energy source, the hydroelectric dam at Owen Falls, generates only 180MW, 100MW below demand.

But the picture is clouded by another project, a Norwegian-proposed facility at Karuma Falls, which would have a maximum capacity of 200MW. Uganda-based Norpak Power says the Karuma Falls project would be cheaper, more flexible and have less impact on the environment. AES has been criticised in the local press over environmental concerns.

Jim Adams, the World Bank country director for Uganda, said the Bank had been invited to provide a report on the two projects.

The analysis will include an environmental assessment, and an analysis of price and future demand. Initial estimates suggest that Uganda could not accommodate both projects, and Mr Adams said the World Bank would not consider any situations which would later require government subsidies.

Potential financiers are watching developments closely.

FINANCIAL TIMES
World business newspaper.

1 Megawatts

Text B

BANKS AGREE FINANCE FOR BALKAN ROAD LINKS

Consortium to fund Croatian motorways

By Kevin Done
East Europe Correspondent

A consortium of international and domestic banks has agreed to provide bridging finance for Croatia's ambitious motorway construction programme to close the gaps in the highway network between the Adriatic port of Rijeka and central and east Europe.

The loans, totalling €68.8m ($77.7m), open the way for work to begin on new sections of the €614m project to complete the 148km motorway between Rijeka, the main deepwater port, and the capital, Zagreb.

The new highway will also play an important role in accelerating the recovery of tourism along Croatia's Adriatic coast, which suffered badly during the years of war in former Yugoslavia.

The loans have been made to Autocesta Rijeka-Zagreb (ARZ), the state-owned company responsible for constructing the toll[2] motorway.

A consortium led by Deutsche Bank is providing a €43.3 million syndicated loan to act as bridging finance until the first stage of project finance totalling between 200 and €300m is completed during the first quarter of next year. An additional four year medium-term loan for DM50m has been agreed with Kreditanstalt für Wiederaufbau, the German development bank.

The syndicated loan has been provided at 80 basis points (0.8) over LIBOR (London Interbank Offered Rate) and for up to 12 months. The terms of the loan demonstrate the increasing readiness of commercial banks to return to lending in central Europe following the crisis in emerging market financing last year.

The project expects to attract funding from the World Bank and the European Bank for Reconstruction and Development..

FINANCIAL TIMES
World business newspaper.

2 A road which drivers pay for as they drive

B Information search

Look quickly at the texts and answer these questions.

1 In which project is a state-owned company involved in the construction? *Croatian motorways*

2 Which project will help to promote tourism?

3 Which project is going to receive an environmental assessment?

4 In which project will the World Bank

    a) provide finance?

    b) analyse the situation and prepare a report?

Vocabulary tasks

A Word search

Replace the underlined items with words and phrases from the texts that have a similar meaning.

1 With the new dam, the country's power supply will <u>be twice as much</u>. (Text A, para 1)   *double*

2 A study <u>referred to</u> power shortages as the main reason for slow economic growth. (Text A, para 3)

3 The press <u>made negative comments about</u> the AES project, saying that it would damage the environment. (Text A, para 5)

4 There will be an <u>evaluation of the environmental impact</u> of the project. (Text A, para 7)

5 <u>Estimates that were made at the start of the analysis</u> suggest that only one project can be supported. (Text A, para 7)

6 <u>Organisations that could be interested in financing the project</u> are waiting for the World Bank's report. (Text A, para 8)

7 The new road will help to promote <u>an upturn</u> in the tourism industry. (Text B, para 3)

8 The loan will be provided for <u>a maximum of</u> twelve months. (Text B, para 6)

9 Investors are showing greater <u>willingness</u> to invest in central Europe. (Text B, para 6)

B Word study

suffer

This word is used in both the texts. What or who suffered in each case? What did they suffer from?

demand

Notice the use of *demand* in these sentences:

a) The hydroelectric dam generates only 180MW, 100MW below demand.

b) The World Bank is preparing an analysis of price and future demand.

Which of these four possible meanings of *demand* is meant in these sentences?

1 an urgent request

2 a request for payment

3 the amount of a commodity that consumers want to buy

4 the willingness of consumers to purchase goods or services

C Understanding expressions

Choose the best explanation for each of these words and phrases from the text.

1 severe power shortages (Text A, line 13)
   a) lack of electric power which is very serious for the country ✓
   b) lack of electric power which doesn't cause serious problems

2 impediment to investment (Text A, line 16)
   a) something that stops people wanting to invest
   b) something that encourages people to invest

3 current energy source (Text A, line 20)
   a) electrical energy source
   b) existing energy source

4 ambitious (Text B, line 4)
   a) something that people think can't be done
   b) something that requires a special effort

5 accelerating (Text B, line 17)
   a) speeding up
   b) causing

D Word building

A facility that is proposed by a Norwegian company is *Norwegian-proposed*. A company that is based in Uganda is *Uganda-based*. Produce similar compounds for these ideas:

1 a company that is owned by the state   *state-owned*
2 a project that is funded by the government
3 a programme that is backed by the Swiss
4 a company that is registered in Australia
5 a syndicated loan led by German banks
6 If a loan of four years is a medium-term loan, what would you call a loan for twelve years?

Over to you

1 Imagine you are a potential investor. Decide which of the two projects you think would be better to invest in. Present your decision, together with your reasons orally or in writing.

2 Imagine you are a banker at Deutsche Bank. Explain the syndicated loan for the Croatian project as if talking to someone from a smaller bank which could be interested in becoming a partner.

3 Either orally or in writing, describe a project in your own country which has attracted foreign investment.

4 Discuss this question: What are some of the problems faced by financiers who invest in large projects in developing countries?

Deflation

Before you read

Discuss these questions.

a) Do you have inflation or deflation in your country?

b) What are the problems of high inflation for consumers and manufacturers?

c) What would you say the problems of deflation are?

Reading tasks

A Understanding main points

Mark these statements T (true) or F (false) according to the information in the text on the opposite page. Find the part of the text that gives the correct information.

1 The UK is definitely going to have big economic problems. *F*

2 The UK's usual economic problem is with inflation.

3 It is difficult for UK manufacturers to compete both at home and abroad.

4 The deflation cycle has already started.

5 The UK has the highest inflation rate of the Group of Seven (G7) countries.

6 The service industries in the UK are in decline.

B Understanding details

Read the last part of the text again (from line 73) and complete the chart.

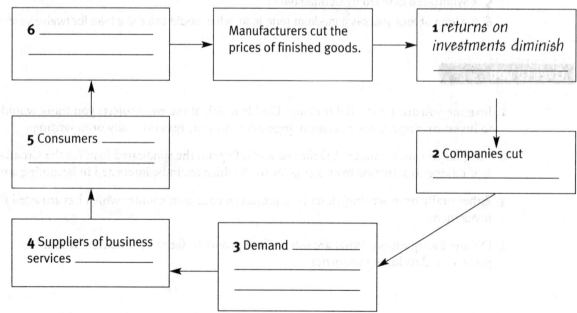

<small>★</small>

NATIONAL NEWS:

DEMAND RETAILING AND SERVICES KEEP ECONOMY TURNING OVER

Manufacturing price falls fuel fears of deflation

By Christopher Adams,
Economics Staff

After decades of battling with inflation, an unfamiliar danger could be threatening the UK economy. Prices charged by manufac-
5 turers for finished goods have fallen over the 12 months to November.

Struggling against fierce competitive pressures, producers have
10 had to cut prices faster than at any time in the past 40 years. Official data show output prices for manufactured goods, excluding food, drink, tobacco and petroleum, fell
15 0.5% in the year to November, the sharpest slide since records began in 1958.

Falling output could tip the manufacturing sector into reces-
20 sion, some observers fear. If that were to happen, a contraction in manufacturing could hit other parts of the economy, causing consumer demand to shrink and dri-
25 ving overall prices lower.

Economists blame the drop in factory gate prices on economic weakness in Asia and the strength of sterling, which together have
30 eroded the competitiveness of UK exporters overseas and made

imported goods cheaper. Domestic manufacturers have had to cut their prices to compete.
35 On available evidence, is deflation a problem for the economy? For the moment, there is little to indicate the possible wider consequences of falling output prices.
40 Recent economic data show 'deflation', or a decline in the general price level, is not yet present.

Overall, the continued strength of the retail and service sectors
45 have been keeping the economy turning over – in spite of the inertia of the manufacturing sector. Consumer spending, for example, is still relatively robust, in spite of
50 slowing in recent months. In fact, the annual rate of inflation for consumer spending on goods and services, excluding housing, was 1.9 per cent in November, higher than
55 for all the other Group of Seven leading industrialised nations. Prices charged by retailers for clothing and shoes have fallen, but these goods represent only a frac-
60 tion of total household spending.

'We're not at the stage where falling prices in manufacturing are having a big effect on demand,' said David Mackie, economist at J.
65 P. Morgan.

Growth in the service industry also remains resilient, with the transport and communications sectors, key suppliers to manufac-
70 turers, enjoying strong demand. Services output rose 0.8 per cent in the third quarter of last year.

However, if deflation were to take hold, the cycle could intensify
75 any decline and be difficult to stop.

As the value of finished goods at the factory gate falls, returns on the investment made by manufacturers to produce those goods
80 would diminish. Companies would find it more difficult to cover the cost of borrowing and cut capital spending.

If demand for plant, machinery
85 and vehicles dried up, suppliers of business services in the transport, logistics and communications sector would also suffer. If growth in real incomes slowed as a result
90 and consumers became more concerned about potential job losses, then household spending could contract too, forcing producers to cut prices further.
95 But economists say this dark scenario is unlikely to happen.

FINANCIAL TIMES
World business newspaper.

C Information search

Look quickly at the text. What are the main causes of the fall in prices thought to be? Which of these are mentioned in the article:

1 fall in price of petroleum

2 economic problems in Asia

3 high cost of imports

4 strength of the pound against other currencies

Vocabulary tasks

A Word fields

Which of the words below are associated with economic weakness?

1 recession ✓
2 decline
3 resilience
4 inertia
5 contraction
6 robust
7 slowing

B Word search

Find a word or phrase in the texts that has a similar meaning.

1 prices charged by manufacturers for finished goods (para 4)
   factory.......... gate.............. prices............

2 people or businesses that sell goods directly to the public (para 6)
   r...................

3 money paid out by each family (para 6)
   h................... s...................

4 profit made by a business compared with the amount of capital expenditure (para 10)
   r................... on i...................

5 interest that has to be paid on a loan (para 10)
   c................... of b...................

C Synonyms

Which words have similar meanings? Match them.

1 producer   a) contract
2 shrink   b) struggle
3 job losses   c) manufacturer
4 fall   d) unemployment
5 battle   e) drop

D Understanding expressions

Choose the best explanation for each of these words or phrases from the text.

1 tip the manufacturing sector into recession (line 18)
  a) cause it to fall into recession ✓
  b) suggest that recession might happen

2 hit other parts of the economy (line 22)
  a) have a good effect on other parts of the economy
  b) have a bad effect on other parts of the economy

3 eroded the competitiveness (line 30)
  a) gradually reduced
  b) suddenly reduced

4 keeping the economy turning over (line 45)
  a) maintaining a cycle of production and spending
  b) threatening the health of the economy

5 take hold (line 74)
  a) disappear
  b) become established

E Metaphors

The writer refers to the UK's *battle with inflation*. What other words in the text make a similar comparison between economics and war?

Over to you

1 Refer to the deflation cycle represented in the chart in Reading task B. Describe the cycle starting like this:

If manufacturers cut the prices of finished goods, returns on investment diminish ...

2 Draw a similar chart to show an inflationary cycle and describe that.

3 The article in this unit was written in 1999. Discuss what inflationary or deflationary trends have occurred in the industrialised countries since then. Were the fears of the economists justified?

4 Either orally or in writing, prepare a short economic forecast for your own country, or for another country that you know well. Describe what will happen, what could happen and what is unlikely to happen. Justify your ideas with reasons and causes.

The work of a fund manager

Discuss these questions.

1 What do you think a fund manager does? Make a list of job activities.

2 Explain what Wall Street is and what it does to someone who knows nothing about stock markets.

Reading tasks

A Understanding main points

Read the text on the opposite page, about the work of a Schroder fund manager. Which of these statements best describes Schroders' investment philosophy?

1 Fund managers work alone to select the right stocks.

2 Investment decisions are best made by groups.

3 Competition between fund managers is the best way to get results.

B Information search

Look quickly at the text and answer these questions.

1 How many ...

   a) committees does Chris Rodgers sit on?   *two*

   b) teams meet in the UK to discuss stocks?

   c) daily meetings does Chris Rodgers attend?

   d) other companies has Chris Rodgers worked for?

2 Write down three activities that Rodgers carries out each day.

3 If Schroders is interested in a stock, what two steps do they usually take to find out more about it?

C Understanding details

Mark these statements true (T) or false (F) according to the information in the text. Find the part of the text that gives the correct information.

1 Rodgers can make his own decisions on which stocks to buy or sell.

2 He buys and sells stocks himself.

3 He was fully trained as an equity analyst before he joined Schroders.

4 He always follows market trends when selecting a stock.

Trading on Teamwork

Team decision-making is fundamental to Schroders' investment philosophy. Fund manager Chris Rodgers explains how this helps him to select the right stocks for his portfolios.

Schroder fund managers such as Chris Rodgers are ultimately responsible for their funds' performance, but Schroders' framework of team decision-making ensures that all fund managers have access to the best
5 research and ideas.

Economists and analysts from our offices worldwide contribute research and recommendations to investment committees, who set guidelines which are adhered to by all fund managers.

10 Rodgers sits on the International Asset Allocation Committee, which determines global targets for exposure to equities, bonds and cash. He is also on the UK Equity Strategy Team that sets specific guidelines that assist UK fund managers.

15 He explains: 'These include ways to control risk, and targets for investing in specific sectors, such as construction or pharmaceuticals.' Within the guidelines, Rodgers has discretion in choosing stocks for his own portfolios.

20 In the UK, two stock teams focusing on FTSE 100[1] and 250 companies, meet weekly. A Schroder equity analyst will present their unique research on a specific company before the team considers information and recommendations from external bro-
25 kers. They subsequently discuss and grade stocks.

Rodgers' daily activities include studying research notes and writing fund performance reports for clients. Monitoring stock market movements and news is a continuous process – the UK dominates
30 the morning while Wall Street tends to govern the afternoon's trends.

'The daily team meeting at 12.15 provides an opportunity to discuss the morning's events and share ideas. Analysts also give expert assessment of company
35 results published that morning.'

When Schroders is interested in a specific stock, the relevant analyst will be asked to prepare a more in-depth note on the company. Rodgers adds: 'We may also arrange a meeting with the Managing
40 Director or Finance Director of the company.

'As Schroders is a large fund manager, we benefit from ready access to most of the companies that we wish to see. We discuss the changes directors are putting in place and how they will affect the perfor-
45 mance of the company in the medium to long term.'

If Rodgers decides to buy or sell a stock, he'll talk to Schroders' dealing room: 'I don't execute the market business myself; that's a specialist and time-consuming role.' The dealers liaise closely, ensuring that
50 the prices and quantities available are acceptable to him.

Like many of Schroders' fund managers, Rodgers trained with the company as an analyst, giving him invaluable experience in researching and assessing
55 stocks. He says: 'It taught me to trust my own judgement. Now, as a fund manager, I have the confidence to take positions with certain stocks, even when the market consensus is less optimistic.

'It's only by going against the grain from time to
60 time that you can add extra value to a client's portfolio over the long term.

CURRICULUM VITAE

Age 38

Education

BA Hons, Human Sciences, Oxford

Employment history

Joined Schroders in 1982 as a graduate trainee.

Spent three years as an equity analyst. Joined the UK Institutional Fund Management area in 1985.

Responsible for 10 pension fund portfolios.

---

1 Financial Times Stock Exchange Index. It follows the share prices of the top 100 and 250 companies in the UK.

From *Schroder Investor,* Schroder Unit Trust Ltd

Vocabulary tasks

A Key terms

Match these terms with their definitions.

1 fund
2 portfolio
3 equities
4 bond

a) collection of investments in different companies

b) large amount of money collected from different investors and managed by an investment company or bank

c) long-term investment traded on the stock market, which usually has a fixed rate of interest for a fixed period

d) shares in a company which can be traded on the stock market

B Word search

Find a word or phrase in the text that has a similar meaning.

1 amount of risk the company is open to (para 3)

e*xposure*........

2 areas of industry or business (para 4)

s...................

3 someone who studies the performance of shares (para 5)

e................... a...................

4 middlemen between clients and stock traders or dealers (para 5)

b...................

5 something that fund managers have to write to inform clients about their investments (para 6)

f................... p................... r...................

6 someone who is responsible for the financial control of a company (para 8)

F................... D...................

7 name of the place where stocks are traded (para 10)

d................... r...................

C Word search

Replace the underlined items with words and phrases from the text that have a similar meaning.

1 Rodgers is a member of the International Asset Allocation Committee. (para 3) *sits on*

2 The guidelines include ways to keep risk to a minimum. (para 4)

3 The team considers recommendations from external brokers. They then discuss and grade stocks. (para 5)

4 Checking stock market movements and news is a continuous process. (para 6)

5 Analysts prepare a more detailed note on the company Schroders is interested in. (para 8)

6 Schroders discuss the changes which company directors are implementing. (para 9)

7 'I don't carry out the market business myself.' (para 10)

D Understanding expressions

Choose the best explanation for each of these words or phrases from the text.

1 ultimately (line 2)
   a) completely
   b) in the end

2 global targets (line 11)
   a) overall
   b) international

3 ready access to (line 42)
   a) limited access to
   b) fast access to

4 going against the grain (line 59)
   a) doing something which the company disapproves of
   b) doing something differently from what everyone else is doing

E Linking

Match the first half of each sentence with the most appropriate second half.

1 Fund managers are responsible

2 Fund managers must adhere

3 Fund managers have access

4 Fund managers have discretion

5 Fund managers liaise closely with dealers to ensure

a) to the best research and ideas.

b) to guidelines set by the investment committee.

c) in choosing stocks for their own portfolios.

d) for their funds' performance.

e) that prices and quantities are acceptable.

Over to you

1 Either orally or in writing, describe your own job responsibilities and daily activities.

   Or (if you are not yet in a job): Find out about a job specialisation in the field of investments and draw up a description of that job.

2 Draw up your own curriculum vitae in writing and then describe it as if talking to a potential employer.

3 If you work in investments, compare the way of working in Schroders with the way you work in your company or bank.

Share review

Discuss these questions.

1 Are the shares listed on your national stock market commonly reviewed for the benefit of investors? Who reviews them?

2 Do you read these reviews? Where can you read them and what do they tell you?

A Information search

Look quickly at the three share reviews on the opposite page and answers these questions.

1 Which company's shares fell sharply at the beginning of 1998 but more than doubled in value in the following year?

2 Which company is preparing for long-term growth following economic recovery?

3 Which company's shares had recently increased dramatically in value but still remained an attractive investment?

B Understanding main points

Mark these statements T (true) or F (false) according to the information in the text. Find the part of the text that gives the correct information.

1 NTT DoCoMo first issued shares on the Tokyo Stock Exchange in 1992. *F*

2 NTT DoCoMo could lose market share to its competitors.

3 The analyst writes that new technology will improve NTT DoCoMo's prospects for growth.

4 Benesse's expansion has been limited because Japan's population is no longer growing.

5 At the time of writing this review, the rationalisation programme to improve Benesse's profitability had just started.

6 Benesse's share price fell in 1998 because small companies were not expected to do well.

7 The analyst reported that Inax Corporation was working hard to increase its value for shareholders.

8 Inax Corporation shares were a good investment because there was an upturn in the house-building market at the time of writing this review.

Schroder Japan Growth Fund plc

Though the uncertainty in Japan is far from over, ther are encouraging signs of recovery. Here, James Salter, manager of Schroder Japan Growth Fund plc, explains the fund's philosophy.

NTT DoCoMo

Sector Communications	
Market capitalisation ¥13,789bn	
Share price in 1998 ¥ 3.9m	
Share price in 1999 ¥ 7.2m	

Our analyst reports NTT Network (NTT DoCoMo) is a subsidiary of NTT (Nippon Telegraph and Telephone) that spun off the parent company in 1992 and is now the world's largest mobile phone operator, with 25 million subscribers in Japan. The company was listed on the Tokyo Stock Exchange in 1998. It raised ¥1.2 trillion from the issue, giving it a strong balance sheet.

NTT DoCoMo is the only carrier providing a nation-wide cellular service in Japan, and enjoys an impressive market share of 57.5%.

Mobile phone use is Japan has rapidly expanded over the last three years, from 8% to 33% of the population. DoCoMo has been at the heart of this growth.

Short-term earnings prospects for the company look less exciting than those seen over the last three years. Market penetration is already high and competitors are threatening to steal market share with a new service which achieves clearer voice quality. However, the launch of the next generation cellular system that will greatly improve data transmission capacity will bring the next growth stage to the company.

The share price has increased by 85% since last year. Even so, the company's share price remains attractive when compared to other international phone companies.

Benesse

Sector Services	
Market capitalisation ¥542bn	
Share price in 1998 ¥4,016	
Share price in 1999 ¥10,200	

Our analyst reports Benesse is the largest Japanese provider of correspondence education. It provides services to four million subscribers, to schoolchildren and adults. The company also operates language schools and a publishing business.

Despite little increase in the birth rate in Japan, Benesse's core business, correspondence education, has shown steady growth over several years. This has been achieved by increasing market share and developing niche areas.

Benesse management teams have carried out a programme of rationalisation that has helped to improve profitability. They are now embarked upon a structured programme to improve cash flow and return on assets.

Shares had fallen sharply in 1998 due to the poor outlook for small company stocks. But Benesse is very shareholder-conscious and generates substantial cash flow.

Inax Corporation

Sector Glass and ceramics	
Market capitalisation ¥205bn	
Share price in 1998 ¥677	
Share price in 1999 ¥863	

Our analyst reports The company enjoys high market shares for a range of housing-related products such as interior and exterior building materials, bathrooms and wash units. The company is also cash-rich, placing it in a strong position within its industry.

During 1998, the company announced an aggressive cost cutting programme, which included reorganising production and the closure of unprofitable business lines. Furthermore, the company has taken an increasing interest in shareholders in recent years.

The recovery of housing demand together with the company's focus on cost cutting has attracted investors to the stock. The management team is proactive, cutting costs to improve profitability, in preparation for sales growth in the longer term. An economic recovery should mean that profits will recover strongly.

From *Schroder Investor*, Schroder Unit Trust Ltd

Vocabulary tasks

A Key terms

Match these terms with their definitions.

1 share issue   **a)** highly specialised product or service

2 market penetration   **b)** process of putting new securities on the market for the public to buy

3 cash flow   **c)** degree to which a product captures a share of the market

4 return on assets   **d)** net income divided by total assets: a key ratio for measuring profitability

5 niche area

                              e) amount of money made by a business which it can use for investment

B Understanding expressions

Choose the best explanation for each of these words or phrases from the text.

1 spun off (line 5)
  a) developed from an existing enterprise ✓
  b) took the place of something that already existed

2 trillion (line 11)
  a) a million million
  b) a thousand million

3 threatening to steal market share (line 29)
  a) likely to take market share from the company
  b) unable to take market share from the company

4 shareholder-conscious (line 71)
  a) not considering the interests of shareholders
  b) aiming to improve the value of company shares

5 cash-rich (line 80)
  a) having a lot of money available to invest
  b) having a high turnover

6 aggressive cost cutting (line 84)
  a) making small reductions in costs
  b) making extensive reductions in costs

C Word search

Find phrases in the text that match each of these definitions. They all refer to strategies implemented by the companies to become more profitable or efficient.

1 dramatically reducing expenditure (Inax Corporation) *aggressive cost-cutting*

2 making changes to production systems (Inax Corporation)

3 stopping production of products that are not selling well (Inax Corporation)

4 planned reorganisation of an industry to improve its efficiency (Benesse)

D Prepositions

Complete these sentences with an appropriate preposition.

1 Despite little increase ....*in*........ the birth rate in Japan, Benesse's core business has shown steady growth .... several years.

2 NTT DoCoMo's share price has increased .... 85%.

3 Mobile phone use in Japan has rapidly expanded .... 8% .... 33% of the population.

4 NTT DoCoMo enjoys an impressive market share .... 57.5%.

E Word families

Complete the table.

verb	adjective	noun
grow	growing	1 .....*growth*.....
expand	expanding	2 ....
recover	recovering	3 ....
attract	4	attraction
profit	5	6 ....

Over to you

1 Describe one of the graphs showing share price performance.

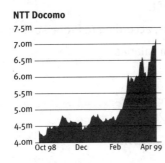

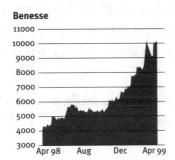

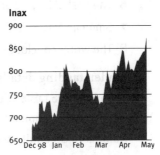

2 Look at the current share prices for these companies on the Internet and describe how they have developed since the time of the review.

3 Choose a company in your country. Find out as much as you can about it and prepare a short review stating whether you would recommend its shares to an investor and why.

Profit from the prophets

Before you read

Discuss these questions.

1 If you want to buy or sell shares, do you read the advice given by the stock market analysts?

2 Do you think it is possible for investors to trade profitably on the basis of analysts' recommendations? Why / Why not?

Reading tasks

A Understanding main points

Mark these statements T (true) or F (false) according to the information in the text on the opposite page. Find the part of the text that gives the correct information.

1 Brokers and university professors agree that stock market analysts are useful.   *F*

2 Research in the 1970s showed that it was better to buy stock not recommended by analysts.

3 In Barber's study, stock recommended by analysts brought much higher than average returns.

4 The best return on investment can be made by investing in small and medium-sized firms.

5 To get good returns it is best not to buy or sell stocks very frequently.

6 The cost of buying and selling can greatly reduce your profit.

7 Small investors can profit from analysts' recommendations, according to Professor Lehavy.

8 The writer concludes that the analysts are worth their high salaries.

B Understanding details

Complete the table with details about Professor Barber's research.

Number of recommendations studied: 1 ..*360,000*......

Number of US equity analysts in the study: 2 ....

Portfolios:

1 = highest rated; 5 = lowest rated

Portfolio 1 Recommendation: 3 ....

Portfolio 2 Recommendation: 4 ....

Portfolio 3 no recommendation.

Portfolio 4 Recommendation: 5 ....

Portfolio 5 Recommendation: 6 ....

Results:

Portfolio 1: Average annual return: 7 ....

Portfolio 5: Average annual return: 8 ....

DANIEL BöGLER **GLOBAL INVESTIGATOR**

Profit from the prophets

Do analysts add value?

Stock market practice and academic theory are sharply divided on this question. Investment banks and brokerage houses spend billions of dollars a year analysing securities, presumably because they think it helps their clients generate superior returns. Yet if you believe, as most academics do, that markets are reasonably efficient, then investors cannot trade profitably on the basis of public information, such as analyst recommendation, since all such data are instantly incorporated into share prices.

Several studies carried out in the late 1970s backed the academics by appearing to show that the average stock which has no analyst following it actually outperforms the average stock that does. However, new research by Brad Barber, a professor at the University of California, Reuvan Lehavy, an accounting professor at Berkeley, and two colleagues, shows a different picture. Not only is their study larger and more rigorous than any previous one, it suggests that following analysts' share tips can be hugely profitable.

The four professors studied more than 360,000 recommendations made by more than 4,000 US equity analysts between 1985 and 1996. Each stock was given a rating – from one for a 'strong buy' to five for a 'strong sell' – based on the average advice of all analysts following it. The professors then constructed five portfolios, grouping the highest-rated firms into one, the next best into a second

and so forth. They then monitored their performance, with stocks moving between them as they fell in and out of favour.

The results surprised even the authors. The first portfolio of 'strong buys' earned an average annual return of 18.8 per cent over the eleven years, beating a stock market index of 14.5 per cent. The last portfolio of 'strong sells' underperformed dramatically, averaging only 5.8 per cent.

To give their research a practical application, the authors then proposed a trading strategy: buy the first portfolio, sell the fifth and you should generate an annual average return of 12.2 per cent.

Unfortunately there are two problems. The first is that the abnormal returns are most pronounced among small and medium-sized firms, which stands to reason since these are less well followed, giving analysts more room

to add value. For the few hundred largest firms, comprising 70 per cent of the US market's capitalisation, the study finds no reliable differences between 'buys' and 'sells'.

Second, to collect splendid returns requires a very active trading strategy, turning over your entire portfolio up to four times a year. The resulting transaction costs eat up virtually all of the extra return.

However, 'that does not make the research worthless,' says Professor Lehavy. Big institutions probably have lower transaction costs and could thus trade profitably. Even retail investors should buy highly recommended stocks and sell those out of favour. The billions spent on analysts seem a good investment after all.

FINANCIAL TIMES
World business newspaper.

Vocabulary tasks

A Word fields

Which of these words and phrases refer to a higher than normal return on investment?

1 superior returns ✓

2 abnormal returns

3 average returns

4 splendid returns

5 extra returns

6 outperform

7 underperform

B Word search

Find a word or phrase in the text that has a similar meaning.

1 financial institutions which act as middlemen between people who want to buy or sell shares and share traders (para 1)

brokerage....... houses...........

2 gains from an investment (para 1)

r...................

3 suggestions to buy certain shares (para 2)

s................... t...................

4 value of all stock market gains over a year divided by the number of stocks involved (para 4)

a................... a................... r...................

5 set of numbers that compares changes in the values of shares with a fixed value (para 4)

s................... m................... i...................

6 policy or approach to buying and selling shares (para 5)

t................... s...................

7 total market value of all the stocks and shares issued (para 6)

m................... c...................

8 commission which you pay to dealers when you buy or sell shares (para 7)

t................... c...................

C Understanding expressions

Choose the best explanation for each of these words and phrases from the text.

1 backed the academics (line 19)
   a) disagreed with the views of academics
   b) proved the theories of the academics ✓

2 more rigorous (line 30)
   a) larger
   b) more thorough

3 fell out of favour (line 48)
   a) analysts no longer recommended these stocks
   b) stocks were no longer quoted on the stock exchange

4 stands to reason (line 69)
   a) is logical
   b) is difficult to explain

5 turning over your entire portfolio (line 80)
   a) making a few changes to your portfolio
   b) changing every investment in your portfolio

D Complete the sentence

Use the appropriate form of a word in the box to complete each sentence.

beat   earn   outperform   underperform   generate   monitor   comprise

1 The return on their share portfolio ....*beat*............ the stock market index by 5%.

2 The highest-rated stocks .... an average of 18.8% over ten years.

3 Analysts .... the performance of stocks over several years.

4 Analysts' recommendations help investors to .... higher returns.

5 Large companies .... 70% of the US market's capitalisation.

6 The lowest-rated stocks .... dramatically.

7 Stocks which had no analysts following them .... those that did.

Over to you

1 Summarise the main points from the article in your own words.

2 Give your own opinion about the value of stock market analysts.

3 Write a short report on Professor Barber's study in your own words. Use the following sub-headings:
   • Purpose of study
   • Method
   • Results
   • Discussion of results
   • Conclusion

Glossary

English	French	Spanish
account	compte	cuenta
acquisition	acquisition	adquisición
advisory	conseil	consultivo
ATM (= automated teller machine)	distributeur automatique de billets	CA (= cajero automático)
authorisation	autorisation	autorización
balance	solde, bilan	saldo; estado contable
banknote	billet de banque	billete
beneficiary	bénéficiaire	beneficiario
bill of exchange	effet de commerce	letra de cambio
billion	milliard	mil millones
board (of directors); Executive Board	conseil d'administration ; Conseil de direction	junta; junta directiva
bond	obligation	bono
borrow	emprunter	solicitar en préstamo
branch	agence	sucursal
bridging finance	financement relais	financiación puente
broker	courtier	corredor
cash flow	marge d'autofinancement	flujo de efectivo
cash machine	distributeur automatique de billets	cajero automático
charge (verb), (noun)	facturer des frais, frais	cobrar, cobro
cheque book	carnet de chèques	talonario de cheques
chief executive	président-directeur général	jefe ejecutivo
clean collection	encaissement simple	remesa limpia
clerk	employé (de banque)	empleado
closure	fermeture	cierre
code	code	código
commercial bank	banque commerciale	banco mercantil
commitment (financial obligation)	obligations financières	obligación
compensate	compenser	compensar
consolidation	regroupement	fusión
consortium	consortium	consorcio
contribution	contribution	contribución
corporate finance	financement d'entreprise	financiación empresarial
credit	crédit	crédito
credit card	carte de crédit	tarjeta de crédito
creditor	créancier	acreedor
cross-border deal	transaction transfrontalière	negocio extrafronterizo
current assets	actif réalisable à court terme	activo disponible
current liabilities	passif exigible à court terme	pasivo corriente
curriculum vitae	curriculum vitae	currículum vitae
dealing room	salle des transactions	sala de cambios
debit	débit	cargo
debit advice	avis de débit	aviso de cargo
debit card	carte de débit	tarjeta de cargo
debt	dette	deuda ; endeudar
debtor	débiteur	deudor
debt service	service de la dette	servicio de la deuda
deflation	déflation	deflación
deposit	verser	depositar
depreciation	dépréciation	depreciación
devaluation	dévaluation	devaluación

German	Polish
Konto; Rechnung	konto, rachunek
Übernahme	nabycie
beratend	doradczy
Geldautomat	bankomat
Bevollmächtigung	upoważnienie
Saldo	bilans, saldo
Banknote	banknot
Nutznießer	beneficjent
Wechsel	weksel
Milliarde	miliard
Aufsichts- und Geschäftsführungsorgan nach britischem Recht; Vorstand/Aufsichtsrat	dyrekcja; zarząd
Schuldverschreibung	obligacja
Kredit aufnehmen	zapożyczyć się
Zweigstelle	oddział
Überbrückungsgelder	pożyczka na czasowe pokrycie braku pieniędzy
(Börsen)makler	makler
Cash-flow	przepływ gotówki
Geldautomat	bankomat
Gebühr erheben, Gebühr	pobierać opłatę; opłata
Scheckheft	książeczka czekowa
Chief Executive	Dyrektor Wykonawczy
reine Einziehung/Eintreibung	inkaso bezdokumentowe (zwykłe)
Angestellter	urzędnik
Schließung	zamknięcie
Kode	kod
Geschäftsbank	bank handlowy
Verpflichtung	zobowiązanie finansowe
entschädigen	rekompensować
Zusammenlegung	konsolidacja
Konsortium/Unternehmensgruppe	konsorcjum
Beitrag	kontrybucja
Unternehmensfinanzen	finanse korporacji
Kredit, hier: Schufa	kredyt
Kreditkarte	karta kredytowa
Gläubiger	wierzyciel
länderübergreifendes Abkommen	transakcja zagraniczna
Umlaufvermögen	środki obrotowe
kurzfristige Verbindlichkeiten	bieżące zobowiązania
Lebenslauf	życiorys
Handelsabteilung	sala transakcyjna
Soll	debet, strona „winien"
Lastschriftanzeige	awiz debetowy
Kundenkarte	karta debetowa
Schuld	zadłużenie
Schuldner	dłużnik
Schulddienst	obsługa zadłużenia
Deflation	deflacja
Einzahlung	depozyt
Abschreibung	deprecjacja
Abwertung	dewaluacja

development bank	banque de développement	banco de fomento
device	dispositif	dispositivo
dividend	dividende	dividendo
document of title	documents constituant le droit de propriété	documento de propiedad
documentary collection	encaissement documentaire	cobro documentario
documentary credit	crédit documentaire	crédito documentario
earnings per share	bénéfice par action	dividendos por acción
European Central Bank (ECB)	Banque Centrale Européenne (BCE)	Banco Central Europeo (BCE)
economies of scale	économies d'échelle	economías de escala
electronic purse	porte-monnaie électronique	monedero electrónico
European Monetary Union (EMU)	Union Monétaire Européenne (UME)	Unión Monetaria Europea (UME)
equity analyst	analyste de fonds propres	analista de capital
European Union (EU)	Union Européenne (UE)	Unión Europea (UE)
exceed	dépasser	exceder
exchange rate	taux de change	tipo de cambio
exposure	risques	riesgo
fee	droits	tarifa
financial services	services financiers	servicios financieros
finished goods	produits finis	productos acabados
fixed assets	immobilisations	activo fijo
fixed term (loan)	terme fixe	plazo fijo
float (a currency)	flotter	flotar
foreign exchange operations	opérations de change	operaciones en divisas
foreign reserves	réserves en devises	reservas extranjeras
fraud	fraude	fraude
fund manager	gestionnaire de fonds	gestor de fondos de inversión
gross	brut	bruto
Group of Seven	G7	Grupo de los Siete
household spending	dépenses des ménages	gastos domésticos
International Monetary Fund (IMF)	Fonds Monétaire International (FMI)	Fondo Monetario Internacional (FMI)
income	revenu	ingresos
inflation	inflation	inflación
interest	intérêt	interés
interest rate	taux d'intérêt	tipo de interés
investment bank	banque d'investissement	banco de inversiones
investments	investissements	inversiones
invoice	facture	factura
issuing bank	banque émettrice	banco emisor
lend	prêter	prestar
Letter of Credit	Lettre de Crédit	carta de crédito
LIBOR (London interbank offered rate)	taux interbancaire londonien du marché des eurodevises	LIBOR (cotización de oferta interbancaria de Londres)
liquid	liquide	líquido
list, listing (on stock exchange)	coter, cotation (en bourse)	cotizar, cotización
loan	prêt	préstamo
long position	position acheteur, position longue	posición larga
long-term loan	prêt à long terme	préstamo a largo plazo
loss	perte	pérdida
lucrative	lucratif	lucrativo
managing director	directeur général	director general
mandate	mandat	mandato
manufacturing sector	secteur industriel	sector manufacturero

Entwicklungsbank	bank rozwoju
Vorrichtung	urządzenie
Dividende	dywidenda
Besitzurkunde	dokument dyspozycyjny
Urkundliche Einziehung	inkaso dokumentowe
Akkreditiv	akredytywa dokumentalna
Gewinn je Aktie	dochód z akcji
Europäische Zentralbank (EZB)	Centralny Bank Europejski
Größenvorteile	efekt skali
Elektronischer Geldbeutel	portfel elektroniczny
Europäische Währungsunion (EWU)	Europejska Unia Monetarna
Eigenkapitalanalytiker	analityk różnic między wartością rynkową towaru a wysokością otrzymanej pod jego zastaw pożyczki
Europäische Union (EU)	Unia Europejska
übersteigen/-schreiten	przekroczyć (ustalony limit)
Wechselkurs	kurs wymiany
Risiko	ekspozycja
Gebühr	opłata
Finanzdienstleistungssektor	usługi finansowe
Fertigwaren	gotowe wyroby
Anlagevermögen	środki trwałe
fester Zeitraum	(pożyczka) o ustalonym terminie spłaty
Wechselkurs freigeben	upłynnić kurs waluty
Devisenhandel	działania na rynku dewizowym
Devisenreserven	rezerwa dewizowa
Betrug	defraudacja
Fondsmanager	Dyrektor ds. Funduszy
brutto	brutto, bez potrąceń
Siebenergruppe, G7-Staaten	Grupa Siedmiu
Haushaltsausgaben	wydatki domowe
Internationaler Währungsfonds (IWF)	Międzynarodowy Fundusz Monetarny
Einkommen	dochód
Inflation	inflacja
Zinsen	oprocentowanie
Zinssatz	stopa oprocentowania
Emissionshaus	bank inwestycyjny
Investitionen	inwestycje
Rechnung	faktura
ausstellende Bank	bank emisyjny
verleihen	udzielić pożyczki
Akkreditiv	akredytywa
LIBOR (Londoner Interbank-Vorzugszins)	stopa LIBOR
flüssig, liquide	płynny (rynek)
notieren / Notierung	tabela kursów dewizowych
Kredit, Darlehen	pożyczka
langfristige Höhe	wysoka wartość
langfristiges Darlehen	pożyczka długoterminowa
Verlust	strata
lukrativ	dochodowy
Geschäftsführer	dyrektor zarządzający
Bankvollmacht	mandat (zlecenie)
herstellender Sektor	sektor przemysłowy

market capitalisation	capitalisation boursière	valor de mercado del capital emitido
market penetration	pénétration du marché	penetración en el mercado
maturity	échéance	vencimiento
merger	fusion	fusión
monetary policy	politique monétaire	política monetaria
money transmission system	système de transfert de fonds	sistema de transferencia monetaria
mortgage	prêt hypothécaire	hipoteca
multinational	multinationale	multinacional
net	net	neto
net interest margin	marge nette de l'intérêt	margen de interés neto
niche	entreprise qui se positionne sur un créneau spécialisé	especialista
obligation	obligation	obligación
operating cost	frais d'exploitation	gasto de explotación
operating profit	bénéfice d'exploitation	beneficio de explotación
outperform	avoir un meilleur comportement	aventajar
output	sortie	salida
overdraft facility	autorisation de découvert	servicio de sobregiro
owe	devoir	deber
parent company	société mère	sociedad matriz
participant	participant	participante
payment	paiement	pago
personal customer	client particulier	cliente personal
PIN	code confidentiel	NIP
portfolio	portefeuille	cartera
POS (Point of Sale) device	dispositif point de vente	dispositivo POS (punto de venta)
price stability	stabilité des prix	estabilidad de precios
profit	profits	beneficio
profitability ratio	ratio de rentabilité	coeficiente de rentabilidad
provision	provision	medida
rationalisation	rationalisation	racionalización
recession	récession	recesión
recovery	rétablissement, redressement	recuperación
refund	remboursement	devolución
repay	rembourser	reembolsar
reserves	réserves	reservas
restructuring	restructuration	reestructuración
retail banking	banques de réseau	servicios bancarios para consumidores
retail sector	secteur de la vente au détail	sector minorista
retailer	détaillant	minorista
retained profit	bénéfices non distribués	beneficios retenidos
retire	prendre sa retraite	retirarse
return on assets	rentabilité des actifs	rendimiento del capital
return on investment	rendement des capitaux investis	recuperación de la inversión
salary	salaire	sueldo
savings	épargne	ahorros
sector	secteur	sector
securities	valeurs	valores
security (collateral on loan)	garantie	garantía
service sector	secteur tertiaire	sector terciario
settlement	accord	acuerdo
share	action	acción
share capital	capital-actions	capital social
shareholder	actionnaire	accionista

Börsenwert	kapitalizacja rynku
Marktanteil	penetracja rynku
Fälligkeit	termin płatności
Fusion	fuzja
Geldpolitik	polityka monetarna
Zahlungsverkehrssystem	system przelewu pieniędzy
Hypothek	pożyczka hipoteczna
multinational	międzynarodowy
netto	netto
Nettozinsgewinnspanne	marża oprocentowania netto
Nische	nisza
Verbindlichkeit	obligacja
Betriebskosten	koszty eksploatacji
Betriebsgewinn	dochody eksploatacyjne
besser abschneiden	przynosić lepsze dochody od oczekiwanych
Produktion	wydajność
Überziehungskredit	przekroczenie kredytu (uzgodnione z bankiem)
schulden	winien
Muttergesellschaft	firma macierzysta
Teilnehmer	uczestnik
Zahlung	płatność
Privatkunde	klient osobisty
Geheimzahl	osobisty numer identyfikacyjny
Portfolio	portfolio
Scannerkassenvorrichtung	urządzenie POS (punkt sprzedaży)
Preisstabilität	stabilność cenowa
Profit	zysk
Ertragskraft-Verhältnis	stopa zysku
Rückstellungen vornehmen	klauzula
Rationalisierung	racjonalizacja
Rezession	recesja
Aufschwung	poprawa
Rückerstattung	zwrot kosztów
zurückzahlen	spłacać
Reserven	rezerwy
Umstrukturierung	restrukturyzacja
Privatkundengeschäft	bankowość handlowa
Einzelhandelssektor	sektor detaliczny
Einzelhändler	detalista
Gewinnrücklage	zatrzymane zyski
in den Ruhestand treten	przejść na emeryturę
Gesamtkapitalrentabilität	zysk z aktywów
Kapitalrendite	zysk z inwestycji
Einkommen	pensja
Ersparnisse	oszczędności
Sektor	sektor
Wertpapiere	papiery wartościowe
akzessorische Sicherheit	zabezpieczenie, gwarancja, poręczenie
Dienstleistungssektor	sektor usługowy
Begleichung	uregulowanie płatności
Aktie	akcja
Aktienkapital	kapitał akcyjny
Aktionär	akcjonariusz

share issue	émission d'action	emisión de acciones
smart card	carte à mémoire	tarjeta de pago electrónica
statute	statuts	estatuto
stock (1) = share; (2) items held in store ready for use	(1) valeur; (2) stock	(1) acción; (2) existencias
stock market index	indice des valeurs boursières	índice de Bolsa
subscriber	cotisant	suscriptor
subsidiary	filiale	subsidiario
subsidies	subventions	subvenciones
supervision	surveillance	supervisión
syndicated loan	prêt consenti par un consortium de banques	préstamo sindicado
takeover	prise de controle	absorción
tariff	tarif	tarifa
tax	impôts	impuesto
terms and conditions	modalités	plazos y disposiciones
total shareholder return	rentabilité totale pour les actionnaires	rendimiento total de los accionistas
trade deficit	déficit de la balance commerciale	déficit de la balanza comercial
trade surplus	excédent de la balance commerciale	superávit de la balanza comercial
trading strategy	stratégie commerciale	estrategia comercial
transaction	transaction	transacción
treasury bill	bon du trésor	letra del tesoro
trillion	trillion (Brit), billion (Am.)	billón
turnover	chiffre d'affaires	facturación
underperform	ne pas se comporter comme prévu	actuar por debajo de sus posibilidades
unemployment	chômage	desempleo
unit cost	prix de revient unitaire	coste unitario
value	valeur	valor
value date	date de valeur	fecha de valor
volume	volume	volumen
wallet	portefeuille	cartera
withdraw	retirer	retirar
World Bank	Banque Mondial	Banco Mundial

Aktienemission	emisja akcji
Chipkarte/Smart Card	Karta Smart
Gesetz	statut
(1) Aktie; (2) Lagerbestand	(1) akcja; (2) zasoby
Börsenindex	indeks rynku walorów
Zeichner	subskrybent
Tochtergesellschaft	przedsiębiorstwo zależne
Subventionen	subsydia
Aufsicht	nadzór
Gemeinschaftsdarlehen	pożyczka jednoczesna
Übernahme	przejęcie
Tarif	taryfa
Steuer	podatek
Geschäftsbedingungen	warunki umowy
Gesamtrendite für Aktionäre	całkowity dochód dla akcjonariuszy
Handelsdefizit	deficyt bilansu handlowego
Handelsüberschuß	nadwyżka handlowa
Handelsstrategie	strategia handlo
Transaktion	transakcja
Schatzwechsel	bilet skarbowy
Billion	trylion
Umsatz	obrót
unter etwas abschneiden	przynosić rezultaty gorsze od oczekiwanych
Arbeitslosigkeit	bezrobocie
Stückkosten	koszt jednostkowy
Wert	wartość, wyceniać
Valutatag	data wyceny
Menge	wolumen
Brieftasche	portfel
abheben	wycofać
Weltbank	Bank Światowy

Key

Reading tasks

A 2 a   **3** d   **4** f   **5** b   **6** c
B 2 T   **3** T   **4** T   **5** F   **6** F
  7 F   **8** T

Vocabulary tasks

A 2 c   **3** d   **4** f   **5** a   **6** c
B 2 complete   **3** current   **4** instantaneously   **5** funds   **6** without charge
C 2 safe   **3** simple   **4** expensive   **5** convenient   **6** friendly
D 2 a   **3** a   **4** b   **5** b   **6** b
E 2 g   **3** d   **4** e   **5** c   **6** h   **7** a   **8** f
E 2 g   **3** d   **4** c   **5** c   **6** h   **7** a   **8** f
F 2 fill in a form   **3** transfer funds   **4** accept cheques   **5** submit an application
  6 open an account   **7** deduct tax   **8** protect ... assets

Reading tasks

A 2 c   **3** f   **4** b   **5** e   **6** d
B 2 T   **3** F   **4** F   **5** T   **6** T   **7** F   **8** F   **9** T

Vocabulary tasks

A *participants*: bank, service provider
  devices: telephone, POS device, reader
  benefits: cost-savings, security, flexibility
  transactions: withdraw, deposit, transfer money

B 2 POS device   **3** service provider   **4** deposit
  5 flexibility / convenience   **6** transfer money
C 2 digits   **3** settled   **4** balance
D 2 complements **3** cash machine   **4** lightweight   **5** log
E

	money	goods or services	your bank account	the balance of your account
pay for		✓		
access	✓		✓	✓
withdraw	✓			
read				✓
deposit	✓			
transfer	✓			
check			✓	✓

F 2 b   **3** e   **4** f   **5** a   **6** c

Unit 3 Reading tasks

A	**2** T	**3** F	**4** T	**5** F	**6** T	**7** T
	8 F	**9** F	**10** T	**11** F	**12** T	

B	**2** No	**3** No	**4** No	**5** Yes	**6** Yes

Vocabulary tasks

A	**2** lend	**3** debt	**4** repay	**5** borrowed	**6** owed	
B	**2** term	**3** current rate	**4** withdrawal	**5** savings	**6** afford	
C	**2** a	**3** b	**4** b	**5** a	**6** a	**7** b
D	**2** a	**3** d	**4** b			

E 1 earned interest **2** set up a loan facility
3 pay off her mortgage **4** running his finances

F	**2** overall	**3** additional	**4** credit	**5** repay

Unit 4 Before you read

2 *loan*: money lent on condition that it is paid back by an agreed date, usually with interest

overdraft: a loan made by a bank to a customer on the basis that he or she may take out more money than is actually in a bank account

Reading tasks

1 b) T	**c)** F	**d)** F	**e)** F	**f)** T	**g)** F
2 b) F	**c)** T	**d)** F	**e)** T	**f)** F	

Vocabulary tasks

A 1 b) maintain **c)** contribution **d)** equivalent
2 b) per annum **c)** fee **d)** premises

B	**2** b	**3** b	**4** a		
C	**2** b	**3** a	**4** b	**5** e	

Unit 5 Reading tasks

A 1 b) T	**c)** F	**d)** T	**e)** F	**f)** T
2 b) T	**c)** F	**d)** F	**e)** T	**f)** T

Vocabulary tasks

A	**2** h	**3** i	**4** a	**5** g	**6** j
	7 e	**8** c	**9** k	**10** f	**11** d

B 1 *debtors*: people who owe money to the company, e.g. customers who have not yet paid for services

2 *long-term loans*: loans that will be repaid after more than one year

C **2** totalled   **3** Added to this   **4** amounted to
     5 comprised   **6** allowed   **7** overall
     8 Deducting this   **9** left

D **1** **b)** profit attributable to shareholders
     2 **a)** cash-in-hand   **b)** stock   **c)** provision

Unit 6

Before you read

2 **2** a   **3** e   **4** f   **5** c   **6** d

Reading tasks

A **2** F   **3** T   **4** T   **5** T   **6** T   **7** F

B **2** e   **3** a   **4** f   **5** d   **6** c

Vocabulary tasks

A **2** relied on   **3** board   **4** mandates   **5** listing   **6** liquid

B **2** a   **3** b   **4** a   **5** a   **6** a   **7** b
     8 b

C **2** for   **3** of   **4** in   **5** on

D **2** unimaginable **3** minor   **4** non-Swiss   **5** high   **6** traditional

Unit 7

Reading tasks

A **2** executive board

     3 **a)** President   **b)** Vice-president   **c)** member

     4 **a)** payment systems   **b)** banking supervision   **c)** international relations
        d) organisation   **e)** statistics   **f)** banknotes
        g) information systems

     5 **a)** the executive board   **b)** the presidents of the NCBs of participant countries
        c) the presidents of the NCBs

     6 maintain price stability

     7 setting interest rates

     8 ECB's governing council

B **2** T   **3** T   **4** T   **5** F   **6** F

Vocabulary tasks

A *organisational structure*: be composed of, be run by, be headed by
    responsibility: be in charge of, undertake, ensure
    change: shift, transition, take over from,
    comparison: relatively small,

B **2** c   **3** a   **4** e   **5** b

C **2** g   **3** b   **4** c   **5** a   **6** e   **7** f

D **2** advisory   **3** participant   **4** participation   **5** (de)stabilising   **6** influence

Unit 8 Reading tasks

A 2 F   **3** T   **4** T   **5** F   **6** F   **7** T
  8 T

B 1 d, f, h, i

  2 d, e

Vocabulary tasks

A 2 a   **3** b   **4** d

B 2 mature   **3** expand   **4** around   **5** decade   **6** handled   **7** run
  8 rivals   **9** swap   **10** fat

C 2 a   **3** a   **4** a   **5** b   **6** a

D 2 branch network   **3** peak   **4** consumer-friendly
  5 credited   **6** leading banks

E 1 b   **2** c   **3** d   **4** a

Unit 9 Before you read

1 a) When two companies, often equal in size, combine to form one new company.
  b) acquisition, takeover

Reading tasks

A 1 b) F   **c)** F   **d)** T   **e)** T   **f)** F
  g) F   **h)** T   **i)** T   **j)** T   **k)** T

  2 (I) Mergers in investment banking, (II) Mergers in retail banking

  3 retail, commercial, investment

Vocabulary tasks

A 2 a   **3** g   **4** h   **5** e   **6** f
  7 d   **8** b   **9** i

B 2 merger mania   **3** cross-border deal   **4** economies ... scale

C *Words meaning to get bigger*: stretch, spiral
  Words meaning to get smaller: scale back, shrink, decline, fall

D 2 a   **3** b   **4** b   **5** b   **6** a
  7 b   **8** a   **9** b   **10** a

Unit 10 Before you read

2 c) *Rise*: regain, boost, gain
  Fall: move lower, drop, weaken, decline, slide

Reading tasks

A 2 T   **3** T   **4** T   **5** F   **6** T
  7 T   **8** F   **9** F   **10** T

B 4, 6, 8, 9

C

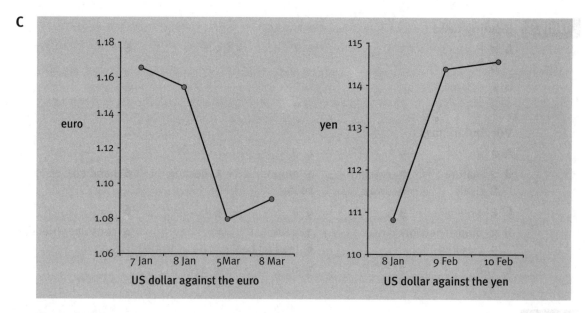

US dollar against the euro

US dollar against the yen

Vocabulary tasks

A 2 capital flows   **3** long dollar position   **4** low point
  5 retail sales figures

B 2 data   **3** released   **4** press   **5** significant

C 2 a   **3** b   **4** a   **5** a   **6** b   **7** a

Unit 11

Reading tasks

A 2 para c   **3** para f   **4** para a   **5** para e   **6** para b

B 2 F   **3** F   **4** T   **5** F   **6** F

Vocabulary tasks

A 2 debit advice   **3** value date   **4** refund   **5** tariff

B 2 f   **3** b   **4** h   **5** a   **6** d
  7 c   **8** g

C 2 production   **3** advice   **4** delivery   **5** daily

D 2 f   **3** a   **4** b   **5** c   **6** e

E 2 d   **3** a   **4** f   **5** c   **6** e

Unit 12

Reading tasks

A 2 Bills for collection   **3** Documentary credit   **4** Advance payment

B 2 F   **3** T   **4** F   **5** T   **6** F
  7 T   **8** T   **9** F   **10** T

C 2 a, g   **3** b, c, d, e, f   **4** f

Vocabulary tasks

A **2** f   **3** j   **4** g   **5** a   **6** e
    7 c   **8** d   **9** h   **10** i

B **1** undertaking   **2** consignment   **3** intermediary   **4** maturity

C **2** forwards   **3** dispatches   **4** present   **5** accepts; release
    6 dishonours   **7** remit

Unit 13 Before you read

2 **2** e   **3** c   **4** a   **5** b

Reading tasks

A **2** Thailand   **3** Brazil   **4** Brazil   **5** Thailand

B **2** T   **3** F   **4** F   **5** T   **6** T
    7 F   **8** F   **9** T   **10** F

Vocabulary tasks

A **b)** 2, 4   **c)** 1   **d)** 1, 2, 3   **e)** 1   **f)** 1   **g)** 2

B **1** negative growth   **2** predicting   **3** credit   **4** delayed

C **2** a   **3** a   **4** a   **5** b

D **2** crisis   **3** consecutively   **4** creditors   **5** a key component
    6 compared with (*compared to* is also possible)

E **2** reach   **3** granted   **4** meet

Unit 14 Before you read

2 **2** e   **3** a   **4** d   **5** c   **6** f

Reading tasks

A **2** T   **3** T   **4** T   **5** T   **6** F
    7 T   **8** F   **9** F   **10** T   **11** T

B **2** Croatian motorways   **3** Ugandan hydroelectric deal
    4 **a)** both projects
      b) Ugandan hydroelectric deal

Vocabulary tasks

A **2** cited   **3** criticised   **4** environmental assessment
    5 Initial estimates   **6** Potential financiers   **7** a recovery
    8 up to   **9** readiness

B *suffer*: Uganda suffers from severe power shortages.
      Croatia's tourism suffered badly during the years of war.

    demand: **a)** 3   **b)** 4

C **2** a   **3** b   **4** b   **5** a

D **2** government-funded   **3** Swiss-backed   **4** Australia(n)- registered
    5 German-led   **6** a long-term loan

Unit 15

Reading tasks

A 2 T   3 T   4 F   5 T   6 F

B 2 capital spending   3 for plant, machinery and vehicles falls (dries up)
   4 suffer   5 become concerned about potential job losses
   6 Consumer spending drops (contracts)

C 2, 4

Vocabulary tasks

A 2, 4, 5, 7

B 2 retailers   3 household spending   4 returns … investment   5 cost … borrowing

C 2 a   3 d   4 e   5 b

D 2 b   3 a   4 a   5 b

E danger, struggling, fierce, hit

Unit 16

Reading tasks

A 2

B 1 b) 2   c) 1   d) 0

   2 studies research notes, writes fund performance reports, monitors stock market movements

   3 First, an analyst is asked to prepare a report on the company, and second, they may also arrange a meeting with the Managing Director or Finance Director.

C 1 T   2 F   3 F   4 F

Vocabulary tasks

A 1 b   2 a   3 d   4 c

B 2 sectors   3 equity analyst   4 brokers
   5 fund performance reports   6 Finance Director   7 dealing room

C 2 control risk   3 subsequently   4 Monitoring
   5 in-depth   6 putting in place   7 execute

D 1 b   2 a   3 b   4 b

E 2 b   3 a   4 c   5 e

Unit 17

Reading tasks

A 1 Benesse   2 Inax Corporation   3 NTT DoCoMo

B 2 T   3 T   4 F   5 F   6 T
   7 T   8 T

Vocabulary tasks

A 2 c   3 e   4 d   5 a

B 2 a   3 a   4 b   5 a   6 b

C 2 reorganising production   3 closure of unprofitable business lines
   4 programme of rationalisation

D **1** over   **2** by   **3** from, to   **4** of

E **2** expansion   **3** recovery   **4** attractive   **5** profitable   **6** profitability/profit

Unit 18   Reading tasks

A **2** T   **3** T   **4** T   **5** F   **6** T
    7 T   **8** T

B **2** 4,000   **3** strong buy   **4** buy   **5** sell
    6 strong sell   **7** 18.8%   **8** 5.8%

Vocabulary tasks

A **2** (in this text, but not always), 4, 5, 6

B **2** returns   **3** share tips   **4** average annual return
    5 stock market index   **6** trading strategy   **7** market's capitalisation
    8 transaction costs

C **2** b   **3** a   **4** a   **5** b

D **2** earned   **3** monitored   **4** generate
    5 comprise   **6** underperformed   **7** outperformed

Check Test 1 (Units 1–9)

A Complete each sentence with the correct word. The first letter of each word is given.

   1 If you want to borrow money to buy a house, you should ask the bank for a m*ortgage*.

   2 The bank has raised its interest r................... to 6%.

   3 If you haven't enough money in your account to pay your bills, you'll have to ask for an o................... .

   4 The general running costs of a company, such as electricity and rent, are known as o................... .

   5 The amount stored on a smart card or in your bank account, is called the b................... .

   6 With the Mondex smart card, you can .... funds from one card to another.

   7 Whereas you pay interest on a mortgage, you e................... interest on a savings account.

   8 He has settled some of his debts, but he still o................... $4,000.

   9 Some banks c................... their customers for services, in order to cover their costs.

  10 The total sales during a trading period is called t................... .

  11 A company which owns one or more subsidiaries is called a p................... company.

  12 The strategy formulated by a government or central bank for maintaining the stability of the currency and reducing inflation is called monetary p................... .

  13 A fall in business activity which affects the national economy is called a r................... .

  14 When two companies combine to form one new company it is called a m................... .

  15 Banks have maximised profits because new technology has made them more e................... .

B Choose the best answer: **a**, **b**, **c** or **d**.

   1 Bank customers who are not business customers are called .... customers.

     a) single   **b)** personal   **c)** individual   **d)** general

   2 If you pay by credit card, you have to .... the transaction by signing a payslip.

     a) authorise   **b)** withdraw   **c)** deposit   **d)** transfer

   3 A device which the retailer uses to receive electronic payments is called ....

     a) an ATM   **b)** a cash machine   **c)** a POS device   **d)** an electronic purse

   4 At the age of 60 or 65, people generally .... from work.

     a) withdraw   **b)** resign   **c)** retire   **d)** retreat

   5 The bank granted a loan for a two-year ....

     a) repayment   **b)** rate   **c)** time   **d)** term

   6 The bank withdrew the facility after the company .... their overdraft limit too often.

     a) exceeded   **b)** reached   **c)** touched   **d)** stayed within

   7 The customer signed the contract to show that he .... the terms and conditions.

     a) applied   **b)** admitted   **c)** accepted   **d)** received

   8 Interest is charged at the current rate, which is 2.5% above the .... rate.

     a) lowest   **b)** base   **c)** average   **d)** minimum

9 These rates are fixed until 1 January when they will be ....

    a) re-valued   **b)** reviewed   **c)** retained   **d)** reinstated

10 Possessions acquired by a company for long-term use (e.g. buildings) are called ....

    a) long-term assets   **b)** fixed assets   **c)** current assets   **d)** tangible assets

11 The part of a company's after-tax profits distributed to shareholders is called ....

    a) dividends   **b)** reserves   **c)** earnings per share   **d)** retained profit

12 Money which a company sets aside to cover bad debts is listed in the balance sheet as ....

    a) deductions   **b)** retained profit   **c)** reserves   **d)** provisions

13 People who are owed money are called ....

    a) creditors   **b)** debtors   **c)** lenders   **d)** liabilities

14 Current liabilities are .... from current assets to give net current assets.

    a) added   **b)** divided   **c)** reduced   **d)** deducted

15 The costs of salaries, heating, lighting and rent .... to 2.4 million.

    a) amounted   **b)** added   **c)** totalled   **d)** summed up

16 Measuring the profitability of a company by dividing the profit attributable to shareholders by the number of shares in issue is called ....

    a) earnings growth   **b)** earnings per share   **c)** dividend   **d)** total shareholder return

17 Stocks, shares and bonds can collectively be called ....

    a) equities   **b)** securities   **c)** gilts   **d)** share capital

18 To sell its shares to the general public, a company must be .... on the stock exchange.

    a) put   **b)** taken   **c)** listed   **d)** drawn

19 One of the functions of a central bank is to .... the activities of banks operating in the country and to make sure that their customers are protected.

    a) supervise   **b)** control   **c)** review   **d)** check

20 When a central bank tries to prevent inflation, it is said to be maintaining price ....

    a) standards   **b)** stability   **c)** rigidity   **d)** uniformity

21 Banks make profit on the .... between the interest received on loans and the interest paid on deposits.

    a) margin   **b)** volume   **c)** net   **d)** value

22 The principle that the larger the company is, the lower its average costs is called ....

    a) unit cost   **b)** capital adequacy   **c)** economy of scale   **d)** consolidation

23 Banks which provide basic services to individuals and businesses through their branch network are called ....

    a) investment banks   **b)** high street banks   **c)** merchant banks   **d)** commercial banks

24 Profits reached a .... last year, when bad debts were at their lowest, and the customer base expanded.

    a) peak   **b)** low point   **c)** decline   **d)** top

25 Lloyds TSB is one of the .... banks in the UK.

    a) chief   **b)** highest   **c)** leading   **d)** medium-sized

Check Test 2 (Units 10–18)

A Complete each sentence with the correct word or words. The first letter of the word is given.

1 Governments control economic conditions according to their m.*onetary*........ p.*olicy*............ .

2 As a result of the recession, the country was forced to d................... its currency.

3 A group of companies formed a c................... to make a joint bid for the large project .

4 As a result of the government's successful job strategy, u................... fell rapidly.

5 The work of an equity a................... is to research and assess stocks and shares.

6 The dollar gained yesterday, following the publication of new employment d................... .

7 SWIFT is a system used for sending money o................... .

8 A document stating details of the goods sold and the amount owed is an i................... .

9 D................... is the reduction of economic activity and the amount of money in circulation.

10 People who act as agents in the buying or selling of shares are called b................... .

B Choose the best answer: **a**, **b**, **c** or **d**.

1 The yen .... yesterday, falling from ¥114 to ¥115 against the dollar.

   a) narrowed   **b)** gained   **c)** loosened   **d)** weakened

2 New unemployment data .... the dollar yesterday, causing it to rise against the euro.

   a) boosted   **b)** gained   **c)** slid   **d)** dropped

3 The person who will receive a payment is called the ....

   a) drawer   **b)** receiver   **c)** beneficiary   **d)** debtor

4 The .... date is the date on which a payment is received by the collecting bank.

   a) value   **b)** pay   **c)** mature   **d)** invoice

5 Once an international payment has been transmitted, it may be difficult to get a ....

   a) repayment   **b)** refund   **c)** recovery   **d)** remittance

6 The bank's charges are quoted in the booklet: 'International .... for personal customers'.

   a) costs   **b)** prices   **c)** tariffs   **d)** expenses

7 After dispatching the goods, the exporter .... the documents to his bank.

   a) demands   **b)** collects   **c)** issues   **d)** presents

8 The exporter's bank then .... the documents to the importer's bank.

   a) signs   **b)** forwards   **c)** remits   **d)** defers

9 The exporter didn't receive payment for his goods because the buyer ....

   a) defaulted   **b)** deferred   **c)** declined   **d)** denied

10 The document which shows details of goods being transported and which entitles the receiver to collect the goods is called a ....

   a) bill of exchange   **b)** document of title   **c)** bill of lading   **d)** declaration

11 A bill of exchange becomes payable upon ....

   a) remittance   **b)** acceptance   **c)** dispatch   **d)** maturity

12 After the war, the country's tourist industry .... badly.

   a) suffered   **b)** bottomed out   **c)** held up   **d)** regained

13 The World Bank refused to grant the loan until an environmental .... was carried out.

   a) estimate   **b)** test   **c)** assessment   **d)** report

14 Short-term loans to cover the period until long-term financing can be arranged are ....

   a) syndicated loans   **b)** bridging finance   **c)** subsidies   **d)** concessions

15 .... means allowing a currency to find its true level against other currencies.

   a) Floating   **b)** Holding up   **c)** Bouncing   **d)** Picking up

16 People or organisations thinking of investing in a project are .... investors.

   a) predicted   **b)** doubtful   **c)** potential   **d)** positive

17 Economists may have to take into account the performance of the manufacturing, service and retail .... in order to comment on the economy as a whole.

   a) segments   **b)** components   **c)** sectors   **d)** groups

18 The government was .... for its corrupt practices.

   a) criticised   **b)** dishonoured   **c)** defaulted   **d)** devalued

19 The person ultimately responsible for the financial health of a company is ....

   a) the finance director   **b)** the treasurer   **c)** the accountant   **d)** the economist

20 Investors are looking for a high .... on their investment.

   a) earning   **b)** return   **c)** growth   **d)** performance

21 When the total value of a country's imports is greater than its exports, it is a trade ....

   a) balance   **b)** loss   **c)** debit   **d)** deficit

22 The value of a company, calculated by multiplying the current market price of its shares by the number of shares issued, is known as ....

   a) equity   **b)** share capital   **c)** shareholder return   **d)** market capitalisation

23 The shares recommended by analysts usually .... the average stock.

   a) generate   **b)** exceed   **c)** underperform   **d)** outperform

24 .... gives customers information about a transaction carried out on their behalf.

   a) An advice note   **b)** A letter of credit   **c)** A treasury bill   **d)** A statement

25 It is essential that stock traders .... to the guidelines set by their employers.

   a) follow   **b)** adhere   **c)** comply   **d)** respect

26 The World Bank uses its .... in selecting projects which it will support.

   a) concession   **b)** evaluation   **c)** estimate   **d)** discretion

27 .... of goods was dispatched three months ago, but it never arrived.

   a) A component   **b)** A contingent   **c)** A consignment   **d)** An output

28 The bank's .... to risk was too great, and eventually led to a collapse.

   a) exposure   **b)** access   **c)** readiness   **d)** potential

29 By issuing a letter of credit, the bank made .... to pay the exporter for the goods, provided that the correct documentation was presented.

   a) a willingness   **b)** a readiness   **c)** a debit advice   **d)** an undertaking

30 The FTSE 100 is an example of a share ....

   a) list   **b)** index   **c)** exchange   **d)** average

Check Tests Key

A **2** rate   **3** overdraft   **4** overheads   **5** balance   **6** transfer
   7 earn   **8** owes   **9** charge   **10** turnover   **11** parent
   12 policy   **13** recession   **14** merger   **15** efficient

B **1** b   **2** a   **3** c   **4** c   **5** d
   6 a   **7** c   **8** b   **9** b   **10** b
   11 a   **12** d   **13** a   **14** d   **15** a
   16 b   **17** b   **18** c   **19** a   **20** b
   21 a   **22** c   **23** b   **24** a   **25** c

A **2** devalue   **3** consortium   **4** unemployment   **5** analyst   **6** data
   7 overseas   **8** invoice   **9** Deflation   **10** brokers

B **1** d   **2** a   **3** c   **4** a   **5** b
   6 c   **7** d   **8** b   **9** a   **10** c
   11 d   **12** a   **13** c   **14** b   **15** a
   16 c   **17** c   **18** a   **19** a   **20** b
   21 d   **22** d   **23** d   **24** a   **25** b
   26 d   **27** c   **28** a   **29** d   **30** b